Street by Street

NEWBU....

HUNGERFORD, KINGSCLERE, THATCHAM

Boxford, Burghclere, Cold Ash, Headley, Highclere, Kintbury, Stockcross, Wash Common, Woolton Hill

1st edition January 2003

© Automobile Association Developments Limited 2002

Ordnance Survey® This product includes map data licensed from Ordnance Survey® with the permission of the Controller of Her Majesty's Stationery Office. © Crown copyright 2002. All rights reserved. Licence No: 399221.

Published by AA Publishing (a trading name of Automobile Association Developments Limited, whose registered office is Millstream, Maidenhead Road, Windsor, Berkshire SL4 5GD. Registered number 1878835).

The Post Office is a registered trademark of Post Office Ltd. in the UK and other countries.

Schools address data provided by Education Direct.

One-way street data provided by:

Tele Atlas   © Tele Atlas N.V.

Mapping produced by the Cartographic Department of The Automobile Association. A01545

A CIP Catalogue record for this book is available from the British Library.

Printed by GRAFIASA S.A., Porto, Portugal

The contents of this atlas are believed to be correct at the time of the latest revision. However, the publishers cannot be held responsible for loss occasioned to any person acting or refraining from action as a result of any material in this atlas, nor for any errors, omissions or changes in such material. This does not affect your statutory rights. The publishers would welcome information to correct any errors or omissions and to keep this atlas up to date. Please write to Publishing, The Automobile Association, Fanum House (FH17), Basing View, Basingstoke, Hampshire, RG21 4EA.

Ref: ML163

Key to map pages	ii-iii
Key to map symbols	iv-1
Enlarged scale pages	2-3
Street by Street	4-43
Index – towns & villages	44
Index – streets	45-48
Index – featured places	48

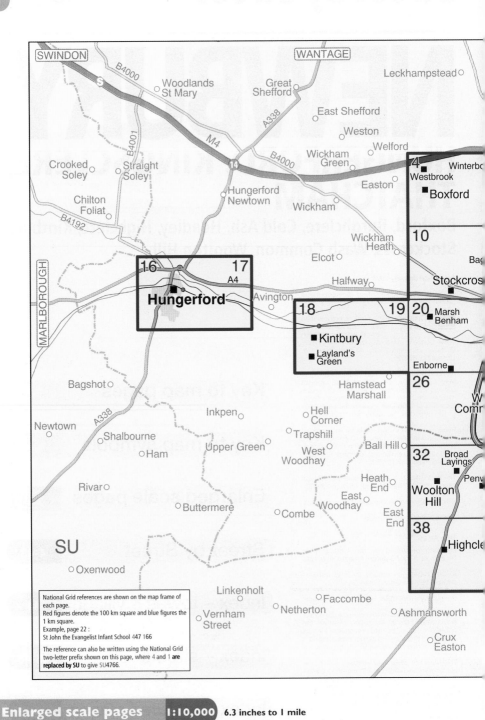

SWINDON

WANTAGE

B4000

Leckhampstead

Woodlands
St Mary

Great
Shefford

East Shefford

A338

Weston

B4001

M4

Welford

14

B4000

Wickham
Green

Crooked
Soley

Straight
Soley

4

Winterb

Easton

Westbrook

Boxford

Chilton
Foliat

Hungerford
Newtown

B4192

Wickham

10

Wickham
Heath

Ba

Elcot

MARLBOROUGH

16

17

A4

Stockcros

Halfway

Hungerford

Avington

18

19 20 Marsh
Benham

Kintbury

Enborne

Bagshot

Layland's
Green

26

W
Comr

Hamstead
Marshall

Newtown

A338

Inkpen

Hell
Corner

Ball Hill

32

Broad
Layings

Shalbourne

Trapshill

Pen

Ham

Upper Green

West
Woodhay

Woolton
Hill

Rivar

Heath
End

East
Woodhay

38

Buttermere

Combe

East
End

SU

Highcle

Oxenwood

Linkenholt

Faccombe

National Grid references are shown on the map frame of
each page.
Red figures denote the 100 km square and blue figures the
1 km square.
Example, page 22 :
St John the Evangelist Infant School 447 166

The reference can also be written using the National Grid
two-letter prefix shown on this page, where 4 and 1 **are
replaced by SU** to give SU4766.

Vernham
Street

Netherton

Ashmansworth

Crux
Easton

Enlarged scale pages 1:10,000 6.3 inches to 1 mile

0   1/4   miles   1/2
0   1/4   1/2   kilometres   3/4   1

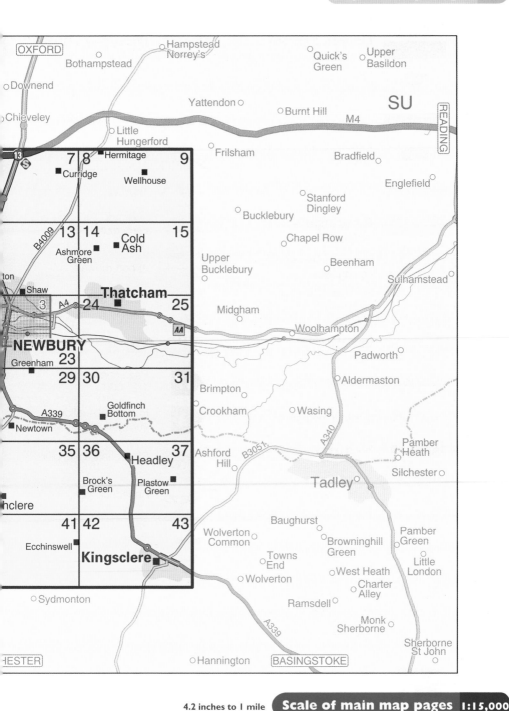

OXFORD

Downend

Chieveley

Bothampstead

Hampstead Norrey's

Quick's Green

Upper Basildon

Yattendon

Burnt Hill

M4

SU

READING

Little Hungerford

Frilsham

Bradfield

Englefield

7 8 Hermitage
Curridge

Wellhouse

9

Stanford Dingley

Bucklebury

Chapel Row

Beenham

Sulhamstead

13 14
Ashmore Green

Cold Ash

15

Upper Bucklebury

B4009

ton
Shaw
3 A4 24
Thatcham

Midgham

25
AA

Woolhampton

Padworth

NEWBURY
23
Greenham

29 30

Goldfinch Bottom

A339
Newtown

31

Brimpton

Crookham

Wasing

Aldermaston

A340

Pamber Heath

Silchester

35 36
Headley

Brock's Green

Plastow Green

37

Ashford Hill

B3051

Tadley

Pamber Green

41 42

Ecchinswell

43

Kingsclere

Wolverton Common

Towns End

Wolverton

Baughurst

Browninghill Green

West Heath

Little London

Charter Alley

clere

Sydmonton

Ramsdell

Monk Sherborne

Sherborne St John

HESTER

Hannington

BASINGSTOKE

4.2 inches to 1 mile   Scale of main map pages 1:15,000

0   1/4   miles   1/2   3/4   1

0   1/4   1/2   kilometres 3/4   1   1 1/4   1 1/2

iv

Symbol	Description	Symbol	Description
Junction 9	Motorway & junction	Underground station
Services	Motorway service area	Light railway & station
	Primary road single/dual carriageway	+++++++++ Preserved private railway
Services	Primary road service area	LC Level crossing
	A road single/dual carriageway	•—•—•—• Tramway
	B road single/dual carriageway	------------ Ferry route
	Other road single/dual carriageway	.... Airport runway
	Minor/private road, access may be restricted	—·—·—·— County, administrative boundary
←	One-way street	▼▼▼▼▼▼▼▼▼ Mounds
	Pedestrian area	17 Page continuation 1:15,000
-------------	Track or footpath	3 Page continuation to enlarged scale 1:10,000
	Road under construction	River/canal, lake, pier
	Road tunnel	Aqueduct, lock, weir
AA	AA Service Centre	465 ▲ Winter Hill Peak (with height in metres)
P	Parking	Beach
P+	Park & Ride	Woodland
	Bus/coach station	Park
	Railway & main railway station	Cemetery
	Railway & minor railway station	Built-up area

Featured building	Abbey, cathedral or priory
City wall	Castle
A&E Hospital with 24-hour A&E department	Historic house or building
PO Post Office	Wakehurst Place NT National Trust property
Public library	Museum or art gallery
Tourist Information Centre	Roman antiquity
Petrol station Major suppliers only	Ancient site, battlefield or monument
Church/chapel	Industrial interest
Public toilets	Garden
Toilet with disabled facilities	Arboretum
PH Public house AA recommended	Farm or animal centre
Restaurant AA inspected	Zoological or wildlife collection
Theatre or performing arts centre	Bird collection
Cinema	Nature reserve
Golf course	Visitor or heritage centre
Camping AA inspected	Country park
Caravan Site AA inspected	Cave
Camping & caravan site AA inspected	Windmill
Theme park	Distillery, brewery or vineyard

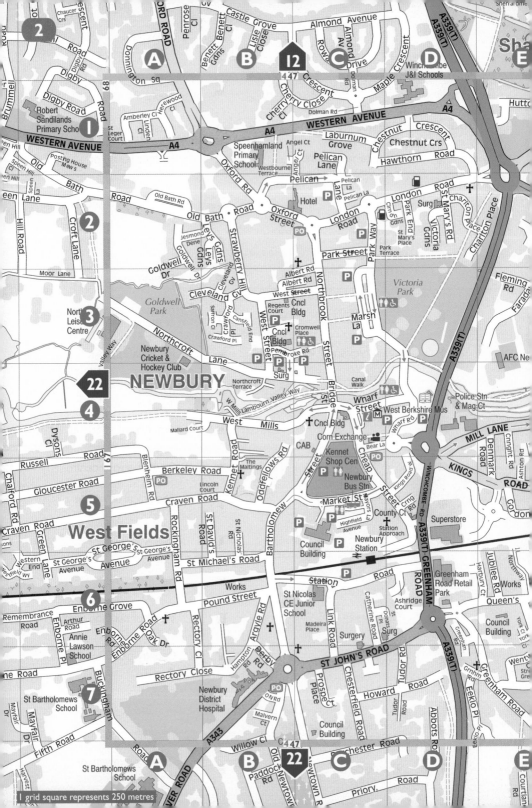

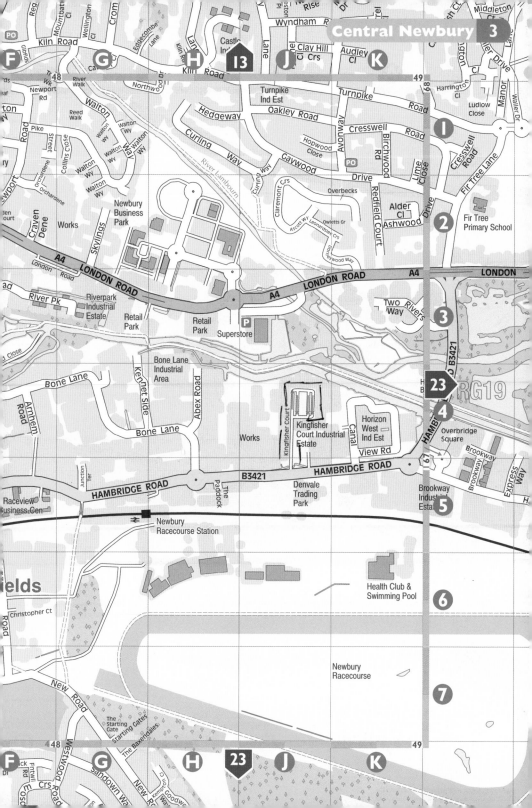

F G H 13 J K

PO
Kiln Road
Mountbatten Cl
Wellington Cl
Crom
Edgecombe
Cl
Glanfers
Ca
Kiln Road
Northwood
Lane

Wyndham Lane
Clay Hill Crs
Audley Cl

48 49
River Walk
Wk

Castle Ind

Turnpike Ind Est
Oakley Road
Turnpike Road
Harrington Cl
Ludlow Close

I

Newport Rd
Reed Walk
Walton
Walton Wy
Walton Way
Walton Wy
Walton Wy

Hedgeway
Cresswell Road
Cresswell Road

Road
Pike Street
Collins Cl
orchardene
orchardene

Curling Way
Gaywood
Hopwood Close
PO
Avonway
Birchwood Rd
Redfield Court
Lime Close
Fir Tree Lane
Drive

2
Fir Tree Primary School

Craven Dene
Works
Skylings

River Lambourn
Claremont Crs
Ascot Wy
Leonardslee Crs
Owletts Gr
Overbecks
Drive
Heywood Way
Alder Cl
Ashwood

Newbury Business Park

A4 LONDON ROAD
London Road
Road
A4 LONDON ROAD
A4
LONDON

River Pk
Riverpark Industrial Estate
Retail Park
Retail Park
P Superstore

Two Rivers Way

3
B3421

Cl Close

Bone Lane Industrial Area
Bone Lane
Kennet Side
Abex Road
Bone Lane

Kingfisher Court Industrial Estate
Kingfisher Court
Canal
Horizon West Ind Est
View Rd

Hambr
B3421

23 RG19

4

Arnhem Road
Junction Ter

Works

HAMBRIDGE ROAD
B3421
HAMBRIDGE ROAD
The Paddock
Denvale Trading Park
HAMBRIDGE ROAD

61

Overbridge Square
Brookway
Brookway
Express Way

Raceview Business Cen

Brookway Industrial Esta
5

Newbury Racecourse Station

Health Club & Swimming Pool

6

elds
Christopher Ct
Road

Newbury Racecourse

7

New Road
Westwood Way
The Starting Gate
Starting Gates
The Baxendales
Sandown Wa
Kempton Cl
Goodwood
48 49

4

A   B   C   D

442   73   43

I

M4

Wyfield M

Borough
Hill

Westbrook
Farm

2   Easton

River Lambourn

Road

77

Hill

Westbrook

3

Lambourn Valley Way

† † School Lane

Winterbourne Road

Boxford

171

PH

4   High Street

5

442   43

Awnham   B   10   C   D

Lambourn Valley Way

River Lambourn

M4

E   F   G   H

45   46   73

I

Lower Farm

PH

Winterbourne

2

Bussock
Hill House

†

Winterbourne Manor   3

6

Winterbourne Road

Winterbourne Holt

4

Boxford
Common

71

Snelsmore Common
Country Park   5

E   F   II   G   Honeybottom   H

45   46

Copse
Barn

6

A   B   C   D

4 46
73

47

Junction

M4

1

Bussock
Mayne

Bussock Wood

Snelsmore Farm

2

72

Bussock
Hill House

B4494

3

5

Home Farm

erbourne Holt

Arlington
Grange Farm

A34(T)

4

71

The Mary Hare
Grammar School
for the Deaf

Woodside

5

B4494

4 46

47

A   B   12   C   D

A34(T)

Snelsmore
House

A339(T)

Shaw
Dene House

Green Lane

Newbury
Showground

M4

E   F   G   H

49   50

veley Service Area

I

Crabtree Lane

Fairrcross
Quarters

Crabtree Close

Fairccross
Quarters

White
Clr

Banf Cl

Clg Dr

RV Cl

Comm Cl

Collins Drive

ariors Ct Road

Faircross
Plantn

Woodlands Cl

Kiln Drive

PH

Curridge

Chapel Lane

Plantation
Close

Curridge Road

LONG LNE

2

Sandy Cl

Sandy
Lane

Curridge
Primary School

Curridge Road

Layleys
Garden

Sawmill
Rd

Marsh
Lane

3

Curridge Green

Rookery Farm

8

ongla

Oaklands

idge Road

4

Snelsmore
East
Common

B4009

LONG
LANE

Cold
Ash Farm

Grange Farm

5

LONG

E   F   G   H

49   50

Fisher's Farm

Manor House

Hatchets Lane

E   F   G   H

53   54   73

Fril

Hawkridge House   1

Lane

ellhouse

2

Brocks Lane

72

Boars
Hole Farm

†

Brockhurst
School

Brockhurst Pre-
Preparatory
School

Marlston Farm

3

River Pang

Holly La

4

Withers Farm   Cole's Farm

71

Tyler's Lane

5

Lane

Hillhouse Farm

Fannys

E   F   15   G   H

53   54

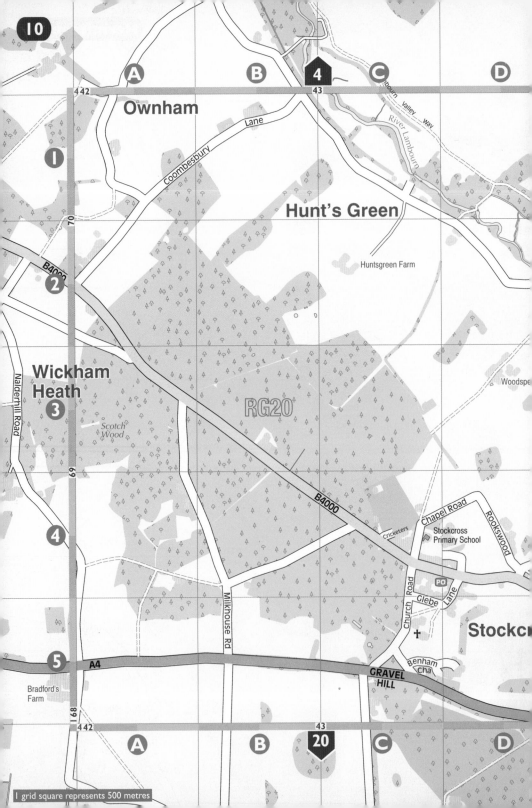

10

A   B   **4**   C   D

442   43

Ownham

Coombesbury   *Lane*

River Lambourn

Lambourn   valley   way

1

Hunt's Green

70

Huntsgreen Farm

B4000

2

Wickham Heath

Naiderhill Road

3

Scotch Wood

RG20

69

B4000

Woodspe

Chapel Road

Rookswood

Cricketers

Stockcross Primary School

4

PO

Church Road

Glebe Lane

Stockcr

Milkhouse Rd

†

5   A4

Benham Cha

GRAVEL HILL

Bradford's Farm

168

442   43

A   B   **20**   C   D

I grid square represents 500 metres

Snelsmore Common
Country Park

E   F   **5**   G   H

45   46

Honeybottom

Copse
Barn

I

70

2

Donni

Lambourn Valley Way

Bagnor

Donnington
Castle

Woodspeen

Watermill
Theatre

PH

Lambourn

Valley

3

12

Lane

Way

River Lambourne

69

Donnington

Dairy Farm

4

Deanwood Farm

B4000

A34(T)

Lambourn Road

The
Sydings

Grove
Road

Grovelan

Grove

5

Sutton Road

Brummell Rd

Cha
Cr

Kersey Crs

Burd

Speen

Station Rd

Winterton Dr

Penn
Road

De Montfort

A4

Manor

Larch

PO

Mr Ct

Kimbers Dr

Speen House

BATH ROAD

68   46   Coxeter
Rd

E   F   **21**   G   H

Battle
Cl

WESTERN

45   46

Church
La

Elmore
House

Speen Lane

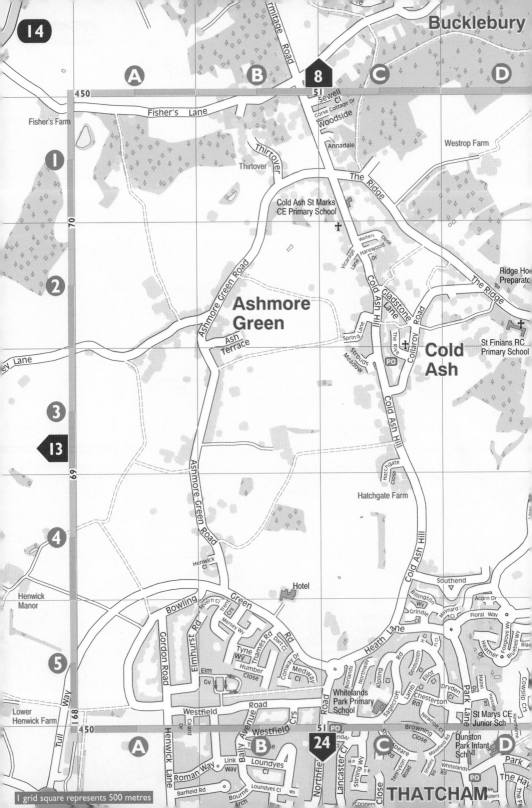

E F **9** G **H** Hillhouse Farm
53 54

I

70

Hopgo
Green

† The
Slade

2

Winch

Broad Lane

Bucklebury
Common

Fannys Lane

Upper
Common

**Turner's
Green**

†

3

Park Farm

Burdens

Heath

Briff Lane

69

Roundfield

Little Lane

Broad Lane Rnd

† **4** Upper
Buckl

PO

Harts Hill Road

Bucklebury
CE Primary
School

Blacklands
Road

Long Grove

Harts
Hill Farm

5

Bla
Co

168

Crs

Chang

Cowslip

Bradley Moore
Sq

Marsh
Rd

Hill

Road

Meadow
Cl

E

Floral

Trefoil Dro

F

Larkspur
Gdns

Simmons Field

Tamarisk
Cct

Pmp

Way

53 **25** G **H**
54

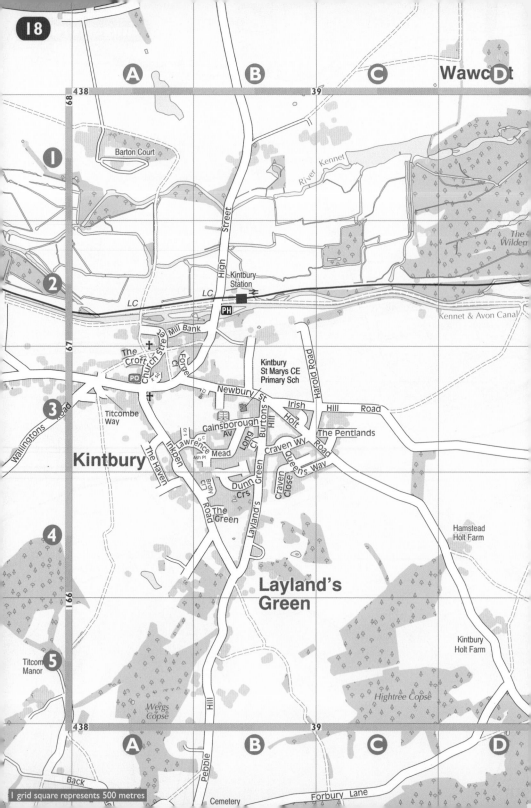

E   F   G   H

Bradford's Farm

I

41   42   68

2

Lane

Park

67

3

Craven House

20 amstea

More Wood

Park Lane

4

Old Lane

Illwills Border

66

5

41   42

E   F   G   H

PH

Hamstead Marshall

Great Holt

Plumb's Farm

20

A4

Bradford's
Farm

A

Rd

B

10

GRAVEL
HILL

Benham
Cha

✝ Stockc

C

D

4 42

68

43

1

PH ⚐

Marsh Benham

2

67

LC

Benham Marsh
Farm

3 ✝

Lane

19

Cra
House

Hamstead Park

Park Lane

4

*Enborne
Copse*

5

Church Lane

✝ Enb

4 42

43

A

B

26

C

D

I grid square represents 500 metres

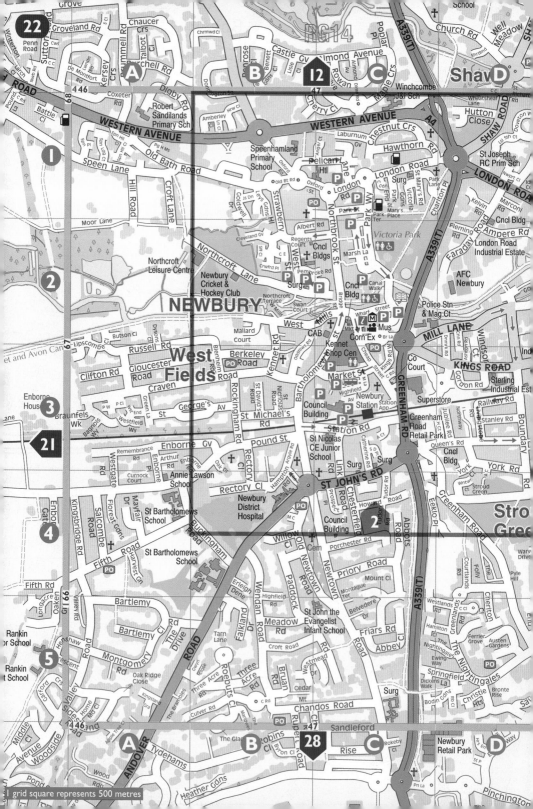

1 grid square represents 500 metres

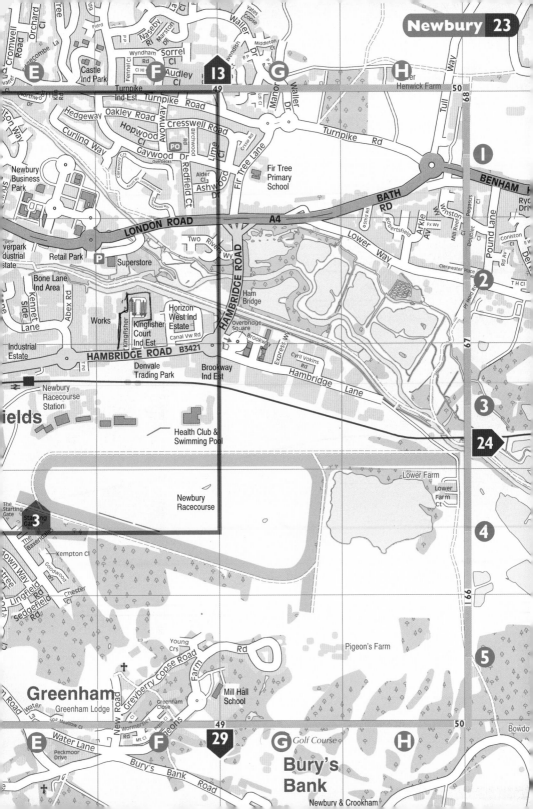

Cromwell Road
Orchard Cl
Tree
Finecombe La
Castle Ind Park
E
Naseby Rd
Marston
Wyndham Rd
Fennel Cl
Sorrel
Cl HI
Audley Cl
F
Yates Copse
Waller
Ivendon
Middleton
13
49
Manor Dr
Waller Dr
G
Henwick Farm
H
50
68

Turnpike Ind Est
Turnpike Rd
Hedgeway
Oakley Road
Anonway
Cresswell Road
Hopwood Cl
Curling Way
Caywood Dr
Clarendon
PO
Birchwood
Redfield Ct
Crow Rd
Ashwd
Alder Cl
Fir Tree Lane
Fir Tree Primary School
Turnpike Rd
BATH RD
Lower Way
Robertsfield
Ostrid Rd
Arkle Av
Winston
Fx Wy
Mill Reef
Pegasus
Pt Head Rd
Doublet
Ryc Dri
Coniston
Rd A
Bel
I
67
BENHAM

Newbury Business Park
London Road
A4
Two Rivers Wy
Ham Bridge
Clerewater place
T H Cl
2

verpark industrial estate
Retail Park
P
Superstore
Kennet Side Lane
Adex Rd
Bone Lane Ind Area
Works
HAMBRIDGE ROAD
Kingfisher Court Ind Est
Kingfisher
Canal Vw Rd
Overbridge square
Brookway
Express Wy
Cyril Vokins Rd

Industrial Estate
HAMBRIDGE ROAD B3421
Denvale Trading Park
Brookway Ind Est
Hambridge Lane
3

ields
Newbury Racecourse Station
Health Club & Swimming Pool
24

The Starting Gate
Starting Gate
3
The Baxendale
Lower Farm
Lower Farm Ct
4
66

Newbury Racecourse
Kempton Cl
Goodwood
Chester
own Way
Lingfield Rd
Sedgefield Rd
Pigeon's Farm
5

Young Crs
Farm Rd
Greyberry Copse Road
Greenham Close
Mill Hall School
Greenham
Greenham Lodge
Water
New Road
Wormersley Rd
SD Meadow Cl
Water Lane
Peckmoor Drive
E
Ptym
Mt Cl
F
eons
49
29
Bury's Bank Road
Golf Course
G
H
50

Bury's Bank
Bowdo
Newbury & Crookham

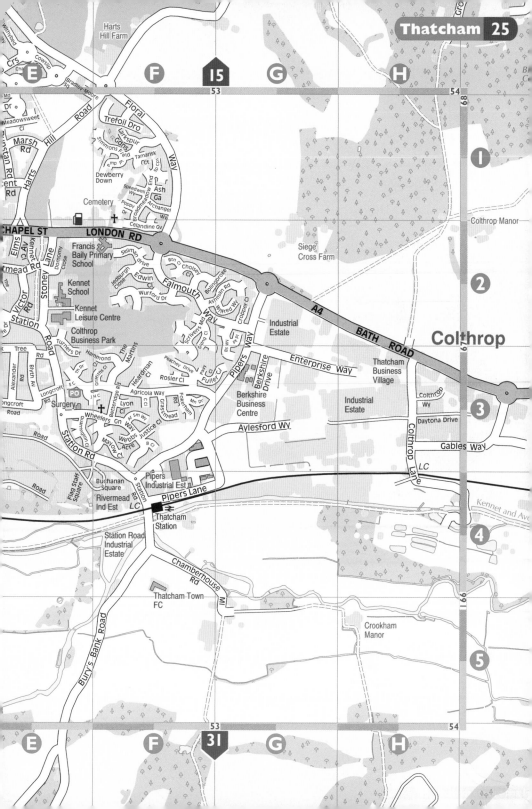

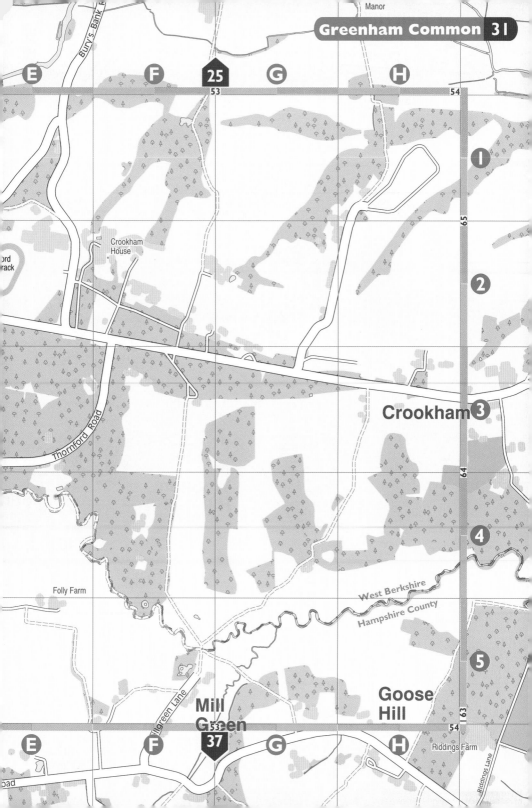

Manor

E   F   **25**   G   H

53   54

I

65

2

Crookham House

3

Crookham

64

Thornford Road

4

Folly Farm

West Berkshire
Hampshire County

5

163

Goose
Hill

Mill
Green

53

37

E   F   G   H

Tilgreen Lane

Riddings Farm

Riddings Lane

Road

54

E

F

31
53

Green

G

Goose Hill

H

Riddings Farm

gs Lane

1

54

63

eadley

Common Road

Durbidges

yres

ne

Milgreen Lane

Hillhouse Lane

Hillhouse Lane

Old Farm

2

62

Kingsclere Woodlands

3

Hillhouse La

Scarlett's Farm

Plastow Green

4

Waits Farm

Works

61

5

Upper House Farm

E

F

43
53

G

54

H

Hall's Farm

mon Lane

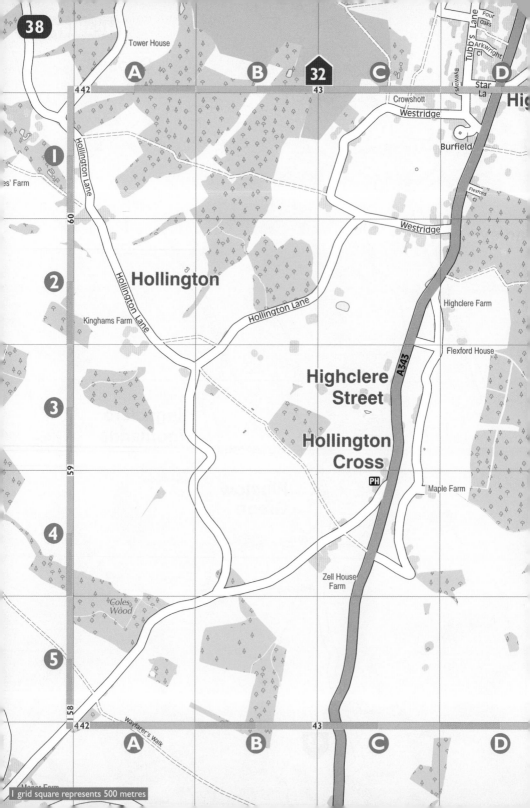

Sandham
Memorial Ch

E   F   **33**   G   H
         45   46

Clere
Wood

Milford
Lake

White
Oak House

West Street

Duns
Mere

The
Temple

A34(T)

60

2

Whitway

West

3

40

White

59

Highclere
Park

4

Highclere Castle
& Gardens

Limetree

Hill

5

Avenue

158

E   F   G   H
45   46

Ivory Farm

40

Sandham
Memorial Chapel
(NT)

Harts Lane

St Michaels
School

Norman Farm

A   **B**   **34**   **C**   **D**

A34(T)

4 46   Spring   47

Budd's
Farm

Lane

Wellhouse Farm

1

West Street

Earlston

60

2

West Street

Ridgemoor Farm

Well

Whitway

Street

Duncroft Farm

3

39

59

4

Hill

5

4 46   47

58

A   **B**   **Old Burghclere**   **C**   **D**

Wa

Palmers
Yard

E

F

35
49

G

H

I

Woodside
Farm

✝

2

Mill
Lane

Cowhouse Farm

Oakfields
Close

Ecchinswell

White
Hill

3

42

Watership
Farm

59

4

Nuthanger Farm

I 58

5

Fossicks

E

✝

F
Sydmonton Court
49

G

H

Sydmonton

Sydmonton
Farm

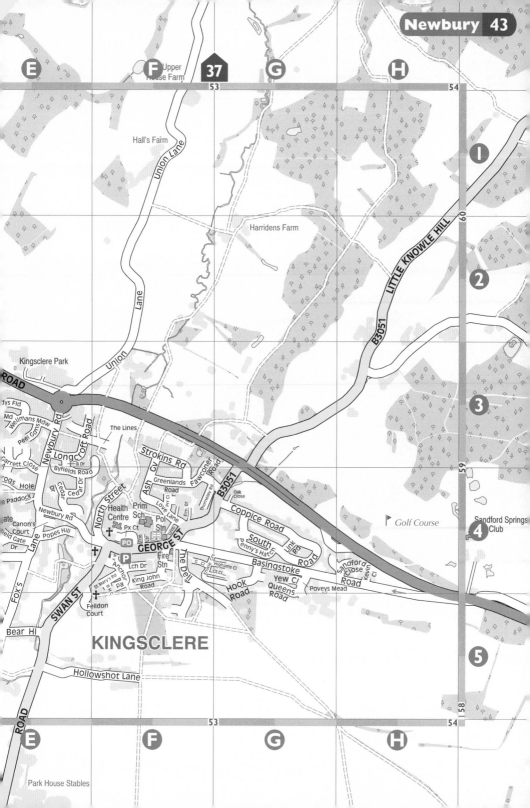

E   F   **37**   G   H

53   54

I

Upper House Farm

Hall's Farm

Union Lane

Harridens Farm

LITTLE KNOWLE HILL

B3051

2

60

3

Kingsclere Park

ROAD

59

Golf Course

Sandford Springs Club

4

dys Fld
Md
Peel Gdns
Wellmans Mdw

Garrett Close
Byfields Road
Frogs Hole

Newbury Rd
Longcroft Road
B Dr
Cedar Dr
Cedar Dr

The Lines

Strokins Rd
Ash Gv
Greenlands Road
Fawconer Road
B3051
Oak Close

e Paddock
Newbury Rd

North Street
Health Centre
Prim Sch
Love Lane
Elm Gr
Thorneley Rd

Coppice Road

Canon's Court
ield Gate
Dr
ate
Popes Hill
PO
P
Px Ct
Pol Stn
Lch Dr
GEORGE ST

Fox's
Lane

St Mary's Rd
Nichol Rd
King John Road
Fire Stn
The Dell

G Cl
G Cl
Highams Cl
L Cl Cl

South E
Penny's Hatch
Yew Cl
Queens Road
Basingstoke
Link Rd
Road

Sandford Close
Kevin Cl
Road
Poveys Mead

Feildon Court

Bear Hl
SWAN ST

KINGSCLERE

Hook Road

5

158

Hollowshot Lane

ROAD

E   F   G   H

53   54

Park House Stables

Ashmore Green ... 14 B2	Earlstone Common ... 34 B3	Kingsclere ... 43 E5	Speen ...
Bagnor ... 11 F2	East Fields ... 2 E6	Kingsclere Woodlands ... 37 G3	Stockcross ...
Ball Hill ... 26 A5	Ecchinswell ... 41 G3	Kintbury ... 18 A3	Stroud Green ...
Bishop's Green ... 30 A5	Eddington ... 16 D1	Layland's Green ... 18 B4	Thatcham ...
Boxford ... 4 B4	Enborne ... 20 D5	Longlane ... 8 A3	Tot Hill ...
Broad Layings ... 32 C2	Enborne Row ... 27 F4	Marsh Benham ... 20 B2	Turner's Green ...
Brock's Green ... 36 A3	Goldfinch Bottom ... 30 C3	Mill Green ... 31 F5	Wash Common ...
Bucklebury Alley ... 8 C5	Goose Hill ... 31 H5	The Mount ... 32 D4	Wash Water ...
Burghclere ... 34 B4	Greenham ... 23 E5	Newbury ... 2 A4	Wellhouse ...
Burghclere Common ... 34 C2	Headley ... 37 E2	Newtown ... 28 D4	Westbrook ...
Bury's Bank ... 29 G1	Hermitage ... 8 B1	Ownham ... 10 A1	West Fields ...
Cold Ash ... 14 C3	Highclere ... 38 D1	Penwood ... 32 D4	Westrop Green ...
Colthrop ... 25 H2	Highclere Street ... 38 B3	Plastow Green ... 37 G4	Whitway ...
Crockham Heath ... 26 D2	Hollington ... 38 A2	Pound Street ... 33 G4	Winterbourne ...
Crookham ... 31 H3	Hollington Cross ... 38 B3	Shaw ... 12 D5	Woodspeen ...
Curridge ... 7 F2	Hungerford ... 16 C4	Skinners Green ... 21 F5	Woolton Hill ...
Donnington ... 11 H4	Hunt's Green ... 10 B1	The Slade ... 15 G2	

USING THE STREET INDEX

Street names are listed alphabetically. Each street name is followed by its postal town or area locality, the Postcode District, the page number, and the reference to the square in which the name is found.

Standard index entries are shown as follows:

Abbey Cl *NWBY* RG14 ......**22** C5

Street names and selected addresses not shown on the map due to scale restrictions are shown in the index with an asterisk:

Bartholomew Cl *NWBY* * RG14 ......**2** B6

GENERAL ABBREVIATIONS

ACC	ACCESS	E	EAST	LDG	LODGE	R	R
ALY	ALLEY	EMB	EMBANKMENT	LGT	LIGHT	RBT	ROUNDA
AP	APPROACH	EMBY	EMBASSY	LK	LOCK	RD	R
AR	ARCADE	ESP	ESPLANADE	LKS	LAKES	RDG	R
ASS	ASSOCIATION	EST	ESTATE	LNDG	LANDING	REP	REPL
AV	AVENUE	EX	EXCHANGE	LTL	LITTLE	RES	RESER
BCH	BEACH	EXPY	EXPRESSWAY	LWR	LOWER	RFC	RUGBY FOOTBALL
BLDS	BUILDINGS	EXT	EXTENSION	MAG	MAGISTRATE	RI	R
BND	BEND	F/O	FLYOVER	MAN	MANSIONS	RP	R
BNK	BANK	FC	FOOTBALL CLUB	MD	MEAD	RW	R
BR	BRIDGE	FK	FORK	MDW	MEADOWS	S	S
BRK	BROOK	FLD	FIELD	MEM	MEMORIAL	SCH	SCH
BTM	BOTTOM	FLDS	FIELDS	MKT	MARKET	SE	SOUTH
BUS	BUSINESS	FLS	FALLS	MKTS	MARKETS	SER	SERVICE
BVD	BOULEVARD	FLS	FLATS	ML	MALL	SH	S
BY	BYPASS	FM	FARM	ML	MILL	SHOP	SHOP
CATH	CATHEDRAL	FT	FORT	MNR	MANOR	SKWY	SKY
CEM	CEMETERY	FWY	FREEWAY	MS	MEWS	SMT	SU
CEN	CENTRE	FY	FERRY	MSN	MISSION	SOC	SO
CFT	CROFT	GA	GATE	MT	MOUNT	SP	SP
CH	CHURCH	GAL	GALLERY	MTN	MOUNTAIN	SPR	SP
CHA	CHASE	GDN	GARDEN	MTS	MOUNTAINS	SQ	SQ
CHYD	CHURCHYARD	GDNS	GARDENS	MUS	MUSEUM	ST	ST
CIR	CIRCLE	GLD	GLADE	MWY	MOTORWAY	STN	STA
CIRC	CIRCUS	GLN	GLEN	N	NORTH	STR	STR
CL	CLOSE	GN	GREEN	NE	NORTH EAST	STRD	STR
CLFS	CLIFFS	GND	GROUND	NW	NORTH WEST	SW	SOUTH W
CMP	CAMP	GRA	GRANGE	O/P	OVERPASS	TDG	TRA
CNR	CORNER	GRG	GARAGE	OFF	OFFICE	TER	TER
CO	COUNTY	GT	GREAT	ORCH	ORCHARD	THWY	THROUGH
COLL	COLLEGE	GTWY	GATEWAY	OV	OVAL	TNL	TU
COM	COMMON	GV	GROVE	PAL	PALACE	TOLL	TOL
COMM	COMMISSION	HGR	HIGHER	PAS	PASSAGE	TPK	TURN
CON	CONVENT	HL	HILL	PAV	PAVILION	TR	T
COT	COTTAGE	HLS	HILLS	PDE	PARADE	TRL	T
COTS	COTTAGES	HO	HOUSE	PH	PUBLIC HOUSE	TWR	TO
CP	CAPE	HOL	HOLLOW	PK	PARK	U/P	UNDER
CPS	COPSE	HOSP	HOSPITAL	PKWY	PARKWAY	UNI	UNIVE
CR	CREEK	HRB	HARBOUR	PL	PLACE	UPR	U
CREM	CREMATORIUM	HTH	HEATH	PLN	PLAIN	V	V
CRS	CRESCENT	HTS	HEIGHTS	PLNS	PLAINS	VA	VA
CSWY	CAUSEWAY	HVN	HAVEN	PLZ	PLAZA	VIAD	VIA
CT	COURT	HWY	HIGHWAY	POL	POLICE STATION	VIL	V
CTRL	CENTRAL	IMP	IMPERIAL	PR	PRINCE	VIS	VIS
CTS	COURTS	IN	INLET	PREC	PRECINCT	VLG	VIL
CTYD	COURTYARD	IND EST	INDUSTRIAL ESTATE	PREP	PREPARATORY	VLS	V
CUTT	CUTTINGS	INF	INFIRMARY	PRIM	PRIMARY	VW	V
CV	COVE	INFO	INFORMATION	PROM	PROMENADE	W	W
CYN	CANYON	INT	INTERCHANGE	PRS	PRINCESS	WD	W
DEPT	DEPARTMENT	IS	ISLAND	PRT	PORT	WHF	W
DL	DALE	JCT	JUNCTION	PT	POINT	WK	W
DM	DAM	JTY	JETTY	PTH	PATH	WKS	W
DR	DRIVE	KG	KING	PZ	PIAZZA	WLS	W
DRO	DROVE	KNL	KNOLL	QD	QUADRANT	WY	W
DRY	DRIVEWAY	L	LAKE	QU	QUEEN	YD	Y
DWGS	DWELLINGS	LA	LANE	QY	QUAY	YHA	YOUTH HO

POSTCODE TOWNS AND AREA ABBREVIATIONS

HUNG ... Hungerford/Lambourn	NTHA ... Thatcham north	RAND ... Rural Andover	TADY ...
KSCL ... Kingsclere/Rural Newbury	NWBY ... Newbury	STHA ... Thatcham south	THLE ... Theale/Rural Re

A

CI NWBY RG14 ....22 C5
s Rd NWBY RG14 ....2 D7
Rd NWBY RG14 ....3 H4
Dr NTHA RG18 ....14 D5
s CI NWBY RG14 ....2 E7
ood Ct STHA RG19 ....25 E2
e CI NWBY RG14 ....23 E4
ola Wy STHA RG19 ....25 F3
Rd NWBY RG14 ....23 E4
I KSCL RG20 ....32 C3
Rd NWBY RG14 ....2 B3
Wy STHA RG19 ....29 H4
urne CI HUNG RG17 ....16 C3
I NWBY RG14 ....3 K2
ders NTHA RG18 ....24 D1
nder Rd STHA RG19 ....25 E3
d Av NWBY RG14 ....12 C5
d CI NTHA RG18 ....24 D1
Ms STHA RG19 ....24 C3
rley CI NWBY RG14 ....2 A1
e Rd NWBY RG14 ....2 A1
CI KSCL RG20 ....43 F4
r Yd KSCL RG20 ....43 F4
er Dro KSCL RG20 ....27 F4
er Rd KSCL RG20 ....33 F1
BY RG14 ....28 A1
Ct NWBY RG14 ....2 B1
dale HUNG RG17 ....14 C1
ford CI STHA RG19 ....24 D3
Tree CI NWBY RG14........................28 A1
d STHA RG19 ....30 A3
ngel Wy NTHA RG18 ....25 F1
e Rd NWBY RG14 ....2 B6
Av NWBY RG14 ....23 H2
ight CI KSCL RG20 ....32 D5
m Rd NWBY RG14 ....3 F4
Smith Wy STHA RG19 ....25 F3
r Rd NWBY RG14 ....22 A3
NWBY RG14 ....23 E5
t Wy NWBY RG14 ....3 J2
urne Wy STHA RG19 ....24 B2
rd Hill Rd STHA RG19 ....36 D1
h RG18..25 F1
v KSCL RG20 ....43 F4
an Rd STHA RG19 ....25 F2
re Green Rd NTHA RG18 ......14 A4
ge Ct NWBY RG14 ....2 D6
Ct KSCL RG20 ....29 H5
r NTHA RG18 ....14 A5
n PI HUNG RG17 ....18 A3
n Rd NWBY RG14 ....2 E5
ood Dr NWBY RG14 ....3 K2
orth Dr STHA RG19 ....24 C3
ton Crs HUNG RG17 ....16 C3
roft Rd HUNG RG17 ....16 C3
I CI NWBY RG14 ....13 F5
n Gdns NWBY RG14 ....22 B5
way NWBY RG14 ....3 K1
ord Wy STHA RG19 ....25 C3
La KSCL RG20 ....34 B3

B

rs Rdg NWBY RG14 ....27 G4
ls Wy NWBY RG14 ....22 A3
Av NTHA RG18 ....24 B1
CI NWBY RG14 ....27 G3
d Rd NTHA RG18 ....24 A1
I HUNG RG17 ....18 B3
rs NWBY RG14 ....27 H1
lomew St NWBY * RG14 ....2 B6
lomew St NWBY RG14 ....2 B6
my CI NWBY RG14 ....22 A5
my Rd NWBY RG14 ....22 A5
stoke Rd KSCL RG20 ....43 G4
d HUNG RG17 ....16 D2
A RG18..23 H1
A RG18..25 H2
BY RG14 ....11 H5
y End NWBY RG14 ....27 H2
A RG18..21 H1
I NWBY RG14 ....27 G2
n's Ct KSCL RG20 ....43 E4
axendales NWBY RG14 ....23 E4
roft Rd STHA RG19 ....24 D3
I KSCL RG20 ....43 D5
NWBY RG14......................................2 C4
rd CI NWBY RG14 ....27 G3
KSCL RG20 ....36 A1
Wk STHA RG19 ....25 E3
olt NWBY RG14 ....27 G3
ere Dr NWBY RG14 ....22 C5
I NWBY RG14 ....12 B5
Gdns NWBY RG14 ....12 B5

Benham Cha KSCL RG20 ....10 C5
Benham HI NTHA RG18 ....24 A1
Berkeley Rd NWBY RG14 ....2 A5
Berkshire Circular Routes
    KSCL RG20 ....21 E5
Berkshire Dr STHA RG19 ....25 C3
Betteridge Rd STHA RG19..............25 F3
Beverley CI NTHA RG18 ....24 C1
Billington Wy NTHA RG18 ....14 A5
Birchwood Rd NWBY RG14...............3 K1
Blackdown Wy STHA RG19 ....25 F3
Blackthorn Dr NTHA RG18 ....14 D5
Blagdon CI STHA RG19 ....29 F1
Bledlow CI NTHA RG18 ....27 H3
Blenheim Rd NWBY RG14 ....2 A4
Bluebell Wy NTHA RG18 ....14 D5
Bluecoats NTHA RG18 ....24 D1
Blyth Av STHA RG19 ....25 E3
Boames La KSCL RG20 ....26 D3
Bodin Gdns NWBY RG14 ....22 C5
Bodmin CI STHA RG19 ....24 C3
Bolingbroke Wy STHA RG19 ....25 F2
Bomford CI NTHA RG18 ....7 H1
Bone La NWBY RG14 ....3 F4
Bonemill La KSCL RG20 ....21 H3
Boscawen Wy STHA RG19 ....25 C3
Botany CI STHA RG19 ....25 F2
Boundary Rd NWBY RG14 ....3 F5
Bourne Arch NTHA RG18 ....24 B1
Bourne Rd STHA RG19 ....24 B1
Bourne V HUNG RG17 ....16 B3
Bowes Rd STHA RG19 ....24 D3
Bowling Green Rd NTHA RG18 .....14 A5
Bradley CI NTHA RG18 ....18 B4
Bradley-Moore Sq NTHA RG18......15 E4
Braemore CI STHA RG19................24 D4
The Brambles NWBY RG14 ....22 A5
Bramwell CI STHA RG19 ....25 F3
Braunfels Wk KSCL RG20 ....21 H3
Breachfield KSCL RG20 ....34 B4
Breach Sq HUNG * RG17 ....16 C4
Brent CI STHA RG19 ....24 D3
Briants Piece NTHA RG18 ....8 B1
Bridge St NWBY RG14 ....2 C4
Briff La THLE RG7 ....15 H4
Brimley Hill Ct KSCL RG20 ....43 F4
Broad La NTHA RG18 ....15 F2
    THLE RG7 ....15 H4
Broadmeadow End
    NTHA RG18 ....25 F2
Broadway STHA RG19 ....24 D2
Brocks La NTHA RG18 ....9 H2
Broken Wy KSCL RG20 ....34 D1
Bronte Ri NWBY RG14....................22 D5
Brooks Rd NTHA RG18 ....25 E1
Brookway NWBY RG14....................24 C1
Browning CI NTHA RG18 ....24 C1
Brownsfield Rd NTHA RG18 ....24 C2
Bruan Rd NWBY RG14 ....22 B5
Brummell Rd NWBY RG14 ....12 A5
Buchanan Sq STHA RG19 ....25 F4
Buckingham Rd NWBY RG14 ....22 A4
Bulpit La HUNG RG17.....................16 C4
Bunkers HI NWBY RG14..................27 G3
Burchell Rd NWBY RG14 ....12 A5
Burdens Heath NTHA RG18 ....15 G3
Burfield KSCL RG20 ....38 C1
Burtons HI HUNG RG17 ....18 B3
Bury's Bank Rd STHA RG19 ....29 F1
Bushnells Dr KSCL RG20 ....43 E3
Butson CI NWBY RG14....................22 A2
Buttercup PI NTHA RG18................24 D1
Byeways KSCL RG20 ....32 D5
Byfields Rd KSCL RG20 ....43 E4
Byron CI NWBY RG14 ....28 B1

C

Cairngorm Rd STHA RG19 ....24 D3
Calard Dr NTHA RG18.....................14 A5
Canal Side HUNG * RG17 ....16 C2
Canal View Rd NWBY RG14 ....3 K4
Canal Wk HUNG RG17 ....16 C2
    NWBY RG14 ....2 C2
Canon's Ct KSCL RG20 ....43 E4
Cansfield End NWBY RG14 ....2 B3
Carnegie Rd NWBY RG14 ....2 D5
Cary CI NWBY RG14 ....27 H2
Castle Gv NWBY RG14 ....12 B5
Castle La NWBY RG14 ....12 A4
Catherine Rd NWBY RG14 ....2 C6
Caunter Rd NWBY RG14 ....21 H1
Cavalier CI NWBY RG14 ....13 E5
Cavendish Ct NWBY RG14 ....13 G5
Cedar Dr KSCL RG20 ....43 E4
Cedar Gv STHA RG19 ....24 C2

Cedar Mt NWBY RG14 ....22 B5
Celandine CI NTHA RG18 ....25 F2
Chamberhouse Mill Rd
    STHA RG19 ....25 H4
Chandos Rd NWBY RG14................22 B5
Chantry Md HUNG RG17 ....16 B3
Chapel Ct HUNG RG17 ....16 C2
    NTHA RG18 ....25 E1
Chapel La NTHA RG18 ....7 G3
Chapel Rd KSCL RG20 ....10 C4
Chapel St NTHA RG18 ....25 E2
Charles St NWBY RG14...................27 H2
Charlock CI NTHA RG18..................15 E5
Charlotte CI NTHA RG18...................8 A1
Charlton PI NWBY RG14...................2 D2
Charmwood CI NWBY RG14............12 B5
Charnham La HUNG RG17 ....16 C2
Charnham Pk HUNG RG17 ....16 C1
Charnham St HUNG RG17 ....16 C2
Charter Rd NWBY RG14 ....22 B5
The Chase NWBY RG14 ....12 B3
Chaucer Crs NWBY RG14 ....12 A5
Cheap St NWBY RG14 ....2 C4
Cheriton CI NWBY RG14 ....22 D4
Cherry CI NWBY RG14 ....12 B3
Cherry Gv HUNG RG17 ....16 B3
Chester CI NWBY RG14 ....23 E5
Chesterfield Rd NWBY RG14 ....23 C7
Chesterton Rd NTHA RG18 ....14 C5
Chestnut Crs NWBY RG14 ....2 D1
Chestnut Wk HUNG RG17 ....16 C4
Cheviot CI NWBY RG14 ....27 G3
Chiltern CI NWBY RG14 ....27 G3
Chilton Wy HUNG RG17 ....16 B3
Cholsey CI STHA RG19 ....25 F2
Christie Hts NWBY RG14 ....23 H2
Christopher Ct NWBY RG14 ....3 F6
Church CI KSCL RG20 ....26 C2
Church Ga STHA RG19 ....24 D2
Church La HUNG RG17 ....16 C2
    KSCL RG20 ....26 C2
    KSCL RG20 ....32 B3
    KSCL RG20 ....34 C4
    NWBY RG14 ....21 H1
    STHA RG19 ....24 D2
Church Rd KSCL RG20 ....10 C5
    NWBY RG14 ....12 C5
Church St HUNG RG17 ....16 C2
    HUNG RG17 ....16 C2
    KSCL RG20 ....32 B4
Church Wy NWBY RG14 ....16 B4
Claremont Crs NWBY RG14 ....3 J2
Clarendon Gdns NWBY RG14 ....2 D2
Clark's Gdns HUNG RG17 ....13 F5
Clay Hill Crs NWBY RG14 ....13 E5
Clerewater PI STHA RG19 ....23 H2
Cleveland Gv NWBY RG14 ....2 B2
The Cliffs HUNG * RG17 ....18 B2
Clifton Rd NWBY RG14 ....22 A3
The Close NTHA RG18.....................24 B1
Clough Dr NTHA RG18 ....24 C1
Coachman's Ct NWBY RG14 ....12 D5
Cochrane CI STHA RG19 ....25 E2
Cold Ash HI NTHA RG18 ....14 C2
Coldharbour Rd HUNG RG17 ....16 C4
Collaroy Rd NTHA RG18 ....14 C3
Collins CI NWBY RG14 ....3 G1
Collins Dr NTHA RG18.....................24 C1
Colthrop La STHA RG19 ....25 H3
Colthrop Wy STHA RG19 ....25 H5
Combe Vw HUNG RG17 ....16 C3
Common Rd STHA RG19 ....37 E3
Conifer Crest NWBY RG14 ....27 G3
Coniston CI STHA RG19 ....24 A2
Connaught Rd NWBY RG14 ....2 E4
Conway Dr NTHA RG18 ....14 B5
Coombe Ct STHA RG19 ....25 E2
Coombesbury La KSCL RG20 ....10 A1
Coombe Sq STHA RG19 ....25 E2
Coopers Crs NTHA RG18 ....24 C1
Cope Hall La NWBY RG14 ....27 F1
Copnor CI KSCL RG20 ....32 A3
Coppice CI NWBY RG14 ....22 D5
Coppice Rd KSCL RG20 ....43 C6
Corderoy CI STHA RG19..................25 F3
Coronation CI KSCL RG20 ....34 B4
Coster CI NWBY RG14 ....11 H5
Cottington CI KSCL RG20 ....43 F4
Courtlands Rd NWBY RG14............22 A3
The Court Yd STHA * RG19 ....24 D2
Cowslade NWBY RG14 ....11 H5
Cowsley Crs NTHA RG18 ....14 D5
Coxeter Rd NWBY RG14 ....22 A1
Crabtree CI NTHA RG18 ....7 H1
Crabtree La NTHA RG18 ....7 H1
Craven CI HUNG RG17 ....18 B4
Craven Dene NWBY RG14 ....3 F2
Craven Rd NWBY RG14 ....22 A3

Craven Wy HUNG RG17 ....18 B3
Crawford PI NWBY RG14 ....2 B3
The Crescent HUNG * RG17 ....18 A3
Cresswell Rd NWBY RG14 ....3 K1
Cricketers KSCL RG20 ....10 C4
Crocus Md NTHA RG18....................25 E1
The Croft HUNG RG17 ....18 A3
Croft La NWBY RG14 ....22 A1
Croft Rd HUNG RG17 ....16 C2
    NWBY RG14 ....22 B5
Cromwell CI NWBY RG14 ....13 E5
Cromwell Rd NWBY RG14 ....13 E5
Cromwell Ter NWBY * RG14 ....11 H5
Cropper CI STHA RG19 ....25 G2
Crowfield Dr STHA RG19 ....24 B2
Crown Acre CI STHA RG19 ....24 C2
Crown Md STHA * RG19 ....24 C2
Crown Yd STHA * RG19 ....25 F4
Culver Rd NWBY RG14 ....22 B5
Curlew CI STHA RG19 ....24 C2
Curling Wy NWBY RG14 ....3 H1
Curnock Ct NWBY RG14 ....22 A4
Curridge Gn NTHA RG18 ....7 G3
Curridge Rd NTHA RG18 ....7 F4
Cygnet CI STHA RG19 ....24 B2
Cyril Vokins Rd NWBY RG14 ....23 G3

D

Dalby Crs NWBY RG14 ....23 E5
Danvers CI STHA RG19....................24 D3
Dark La HUNG RG17 ....17 F2
Dart CI NTHA RG18 ....14 B5
Daytona Dr STHA RG19 ....25 H3
Deadmans La STHA RG19 ....28 D2
Deadmoor La KSCL RG20 ....34 A1
The Dell KSCL RG20 ....43 F4
De Montfort Gv HUNG RG17 ....16 B4
De Montfort Rd NWBY RG14 ....11 H5
Dene Wy NWBY RG14 ....12 B5
Denmark Rd NWBY RG14 ....2 E4
Denton CI STHA RG19 ....24 C3
Derby Rd NWBY RG14 ....2 B7
Derwent Rd STHA RG19 ....24 A2
Dewberry Down NTHA RG18..........25 F1
Dickens Wk NWBY RG14 ....12 A5
Digby Rd NWBY RG14 ....12 A5
Doctors La NTHA RG18 ....8 A1
Dolman Rd NWBY RG14 ....2 C1
Domoney CI STHA RG19 ....25 E2
Donnington Pk NWBY RG14...........12 B4
Donnington Sq NWBY RG14 ....12 B5
Dormer CI NWBY RG14 ....28 A2
Dorneywood Wy NWBY RG14 ....3 J2
Doublet CI STHA RG19 ....24 A2
Douglas Ride KSCL RG20 ....32 C3
Doveton Wy NWBY RG14 ....3 F1
Draper CI STHA RG19 ....24 D3
The Drive NWBY RG14 ....22 A5
Drove La NTHA RG18 ....8 B5
Druce Wy STHA RG19 ....24 D2
Dryden CI NTHA RG18.....................14 C5
Dunn Crs HUNG RG17 ....18 B4
Dunstan Rd NTHA RG18..................25 E1
Durbidges STHA RG19 ....37 E3
Dysons CI NWBY RG14 ....22 A2

E

Eagle Rd KSCL RG20 ....36 A1
Ecchinswell Rd KSCL RG20 ....42 D4
Eddington HI HUNG RG17 ....16 D1
Edgecombe La NWBY RG14............13 E5
Edwin CI STHA RG19 ....25 F2
Eeklo PI NWBY RG14 ....2 D7
Eliot CI NTHA RG18 ....14 C5
Elizabeth Av NWBY RG14 ....27 H1
Elm Farm Gv KSCL * RG20 ....43 F4
Elm Gv KSCL RG20 ....43 F4
    NTHA RG18 ....14 B5
Elmhurst Rd NTHA RG18.................14 A5
Elms Av STHA RG19 ....25 E2
Enborne Ct NWBY * RG14 ....21 H4
Enborne Ga NWBY RG14 ....21 H4
Enborne Gv NWBY RG14 ....22 A3
Enborne Lodge La
    NWBY RG14 ....27 G2
Enborne PI NWBY RG14..................22 A3
Enborne Rd KSCL RG20 ....21 G4
Enborne St KSCL RG20 ....27 E4
Ennerdale Wy STHA RG19..............24 A2
Enterprise Wy STHA RG19 ....25 G3
Epsom Crs NWBY RG14 ....24 A2
Equine Wy NWBY RG14 ....28 D1

Erleigh Dene *NWBY* RG14 ....22 B4
Essex Pl *NWBY* * RG14 ....11 H5
Essex St *NWBY* RG14 ....27 H1
Everland Rd *HUNG* RG17..............16 C2
Evreux Cl *STHA* * RG19 ....25 F3
Ewing Wy *NWBY* RG14 ....22 C5
Exmoor Rd *STHA* RG19 ....24 C2
Express Wy *NWBY* RG14 ....23 G3

F

Fairacre *KSCL* RG20 ....32 D3
Fair Cl *NWBY* * RG14 ....2 C6
Faircross Quarters *NTHA* RG18 ......7 H1
Fairfax Pl *NWBY* RG14 ....13 G5
Fairfields *HUNG* RG17 ....16 C3
Fairview Rd *HUNG* RG17 ....16 C3
Falcon Coppice *KSCL* RG20..........32 D5
Falcon House Gdns
  KSCL RG20 ....32 C5
Falkland Dr *NWBY* RG14 ....22 B5
Falkland Garth *NWBY* RG14 ....27 H1
Falkland Rd *NWBY* RG14 ....27 H2
Falmouth Wy *STHA* RG19 ....25 F2
Fannys La *THLE* RG7 ....15 H1
Faraday Rd *NWBY* RG14 ....2 E3
Faulkner Sq *HUNG* * RG17 ....16 D2
Fawconer Rd *KSCL* RG20 ....43 F4
Feildon Ct *KSCL* RG20 ....43 E5
Fennel Cl *NWBY* RG14 ....13 F5
Ferndale Ct *STHA* RG19 ....24 D2
Ferrier Gv *NWBY* RG14 ....22 D5
Field Gate Dr *KSCL* RG20 ....43 E4
Fieldridge *NWBY* RG14 ....13 G5
Fifth Rd *NWBY* RG14 ....21 H4
Fifth St *STHA* RG19................29 H3
The Firs *NTHA* RG18 ....24 B1
First St East *STHA* RG19 ....30 A3
Fir Tree La *NWBY* RG14 ....23 G1
Fisher's La *NTHA* RG18 ....14 A1
Flag Staff Sq *STHA* RG19...........25 E4
Flecker Cl *NTHA* RG18 ....14 C5
Fleetwood Cl *NWBY* RG14 ....13 F5
Fleming Rd *NWBY* RG14 ....2 E3
Flexford Cl *KSCL* RG20.............38 D1
Floral Wy *NWBY* RG14 ....14 D5
Floreat Gdns *NWBY* RG14 ....22 A4
Fokerham Rd *STHA* RG19 ....25 F3
The Folly *NWBY* RG14 ....22 D4
Fontwell Rd *NWBY* RG14 ....22 D4
The Forge *HUNG* RG17 ....16 C2
Forge Cl *HUNG* RG17 ....18 A3
Four Oaks *KSCL* RG20 ....32 D5
Fourth St *STHA* RG19 ....29 H3
Foxglove Wy *NWBY* RG18 ....14 D5
Foxhunter Wy *STHA* RG19 ....23 H2
Fox's La *KSCL* RG20 ....43 E5
The Frances *NTHA* RG18 ....24 D1
Friars Rd *NWBY* RG14 ....22 C5
Frogs Hole *KSCL* RG20.............43 E4
Fromont Dr *STHA* RG19.............24 D2
Fuller Ct *STHA* RG19 ....25 F3
Fyfield Rd *STHA* RG19 ....24 C3
Fylingdales *STHA* RG19 ....24 C3

G

Gables Wy *STHA* RG19 ....25 H3
The Gabriels *NWBY* RG14 ....27 H2
Gainsborough Av *HUNG* RG17........18 B3
Galley La *STHA* RG19 ....36 D2
Garden Cl *KSCL* RG20 ....43 F4
Garden Close La *NWBY* RG14 ....27 H4
Garford Crs *NWBY* RG14 ....21 H5
Garrett Cl *KSCL* RG20 ....43 E3
Gaywood Dr *NWBY* RG14 ....3 J1
George St *KSCL* RG20 ....43 F4
Giles Cl *NWBY* * RG14 ....22 A3
Gilroy Cl *NWBY* RG14 ....27 G2
The Glade *NWBY* RG14 ....28 B1
Gladstone Cl *HUNG* RG17...........18 B3
Gladstone La *NTHA* RG18 ....14 C2
Glaisdale *STHA* RG19 ....24 C3
Glebefields *NWBY* RG14 ....12 D5
Glebelands *STHA* RG19 ....24 C2
Glebe La *KSCL* RG20 ....10 C5
Glendale Av *NWBY* RG14 ....27 G3
Glenmore Cl *STHA* * RG19 ....24 D3
Gloucester Rd *NWBY* RG14.........22 A3
Golding Cl *STHA* RG19 ....25 F3
Goldsmith Cl *NTHA* RG18...........14 C5
Goldwell Dr *NWBY* RG14 ....2 A2
Goodwood Wy *NWBY* RG14 ....23 E4
Goose Green Wy *STHA* RG19 ....25 E3

Gordon Rd *NTHA* RG18 ....14 A5
Gorse Cottage Dr *NTHA* RG18 .....14 B1
Gorselands *NWBY* RG14 ....27 H3
Gould Cl *NWBY* RG14 ....3 F4
The Granary *NWBY* * RG14 ....2 B4
The Grange *NWBY* RG14 ....27 G3
Grassington Pl *STHA* RG19 ....24 D3
Grassmead *STHA* RG19 ....25 F3
Gravel Hi *KSCL* RG20 ....10 C5
Great Severals *HUNG* RG17 ....18 A3
Greenacre *KSCL* RG20 ....43 F4
Greenacres *KSCL* RG20 ....32 C3
The Green *HUNG* RG17 ....18 B4
Greenham Cl *STHA* RG19...........23 F5
Greenham Rd *NWBY* RG14 ....2 D6
Greenlands *KSCL* RG20 ....32 C2
Greenlands Rd *KSCL* RG20 ....43 F4
  NWBY RG14 ....22 D5
Green La *NWBY* RG14 ....22 A3
  STHA RG19 ....24 C2
Greenways *KSCL* RG20 ....32 C2
Greyberry Copse Rd *STHA* RG19 ...23 F5
Griffiths Cl *STHA* RG19 ....25 F3
Grindle Cl *NTHA* RG18 ....14 C5
The Grove *NTHA* RG18.............24 D1
Grosvenor Lawn *NWBY* * RG14 .....22 A3
Groveland Rd *NWBY* RG14 ....11 H5
Grove Rd *NWBY* RG14 ....11 H5
Gwyn Cl *NWBY* RG14 ....22 B5

H

Halifax Pl *NTHA* RG18 ....24 C1
The Halters *NWBY* RG14 ....28 D1
Hamblin Meadow *HUNG* RG17.......16 D1
Ham Br *NWBY* RG14................3 K4
Hambridge La *NWBY* RG14 ....23 G3
Hambridge Rd *NWBY* RG14 ....3 G5
Hamilton Cl *NWBY* RG14 ....22 C5
Ham Ml *NWBY* * RG14 ....3 J3
Hammond Cl *STHA* RG19............25 E3
The Hampdens *NWBY* * RG14 ....27 G2
Hampdens *NWBY* RG14 ....27 G2
Hampton Rd *NWBY* RG14 ....27 H2
Hanover Md *NWBY* * RG14 ....27 H2
Harbury Ct *NWBY* RG14 ....22 D6
Hardy Cl *NTHA* RG18 ....14 C5
Hardys Fld *KSCL* RG20............43 E3
Harebell Dr *NTHA* RG18 ....25 E1
Harewood Dr *NTHA* RG18 ....14 C2
Harold Rd *HUNG* RG17.............18 C3
Harrington Cl *NWBY* RG14 ....13 F5
Hartmead Rd *STHA* RG19 ....25 E2
Harts Hill Rd *NTHA* RG18 ....25 E1
Harts La *KSCL* RG20 ....34 A5
Harvest Gn *NWBY* RG14 ....22 A4
Harwood Ri *KSCL* RG20 ....32 D2
Hatchgate Cl *NTHA* RG18 ....14 C4
The Haven *HUNG* RG17.............18 A3
Hawthorne Cl *NTHA* RG18 ....14 D5
Hawthorn Rd *NWBY* RG14 ....2 C1
The Haywards *NTHA* RG18 ....14 D1
Hazel Gv *NTHA* RG18 ....14 D5
Heardman Ct *STHA* RG19...........25 F3
Heather Dr *NTHA* RG18 ....14 D5
Heather Gdns *NWBY* RG14 ....28 A1
Heathlands *KSCL* RG20 ....33 E3
Heath La *NTHA* RG18 ....14 C5
Hebden Cl *STHA* RG19 ....24 C4
Hedgeway *NWBY* RG14 ....3 H1
The Henrys *NTHA* RG18 ....24 D1
Henshaw Crs *NWBY* RG14..........21 H5
Henwick Cl *NTHA* RG18 ....14 A4
Henwick La *NTHA* RG18............24 A1
Herewood Cl *NWBY* RG14 ....2 A1
Hermitage Rd *NTHA* RG18 ....4 B7
Herongate *HUNG* RG17.............16 C1
Heron Wy *STHA* RG19 ....24 B2
Highams Cl *KSCL* RG20............43 F4
Highfield Av *NWBY* RG14 ....2 C5
Highfield Rd *NWBY* RG14 ....22 B5
High St *HUNG* RG17 ....16 C2
  HUNG RG17 ....18 B2
  STHA RG19.............18 B2
Highwood Cl *NWBY* RG14 ....12 D4
Hill Cl *NWBY* RG14 ....27 H1
Hillhouse La *STHA* RG19 ....37 F4
Hill Rd *NWBY* RG14...............22 A1
Hillside Rd *HUNG* RG17 ....16 C4
Holborne Cl *NWBY* RG14 ....27 G3
The Hollands *STHA* RG19..........25 E2
The Hollies *STHA* RG14...........27 H3
Hollington La *KSCL* RG20 ....38 A2
Hollington Pl *STHA* * RG19 ......24 C2
The Hollow *KSCL* RG20 ....43 E4

Hollowshot La *KSCL* RG20 ....43 E5
Holly La *NTHA* RG18 ....9 H4
Holt Rd *HUNG* RG17 ....18 B3
Holywell Ct *STHA* RG19 ....24 D2
Homefield Wy *HUNG* RG17 ....16 B3
Home Mead Cl *NWBY* RG14 ....22 A5
Honeyfields *HUNG* RG17 ....16 C3
Hook Rd *KSCL* RG20 ....43 G4
Hop Gdns *NWBY* * RG14 ....12 D5
Hopwood Cl *NWBY* RG14 ....3 J1
Horne Rd *STHA* RG19 ....24 D3
Horseshoe End *NWBY* RG14........28 D1
Howard Rd *NWBY* RG14 ....2 C7
Humber Cl *NTHA* RG18 ....14 B5
Hungerford Rd *HUNG* RG17 ....17 F3
Hutton Cl *NWBY* RG14 ....2 E1
Hyde La *KSCL* RG20 ....36 A5

I

Iden Ct *NWBY* RG14 ....3 F2
Ilkley Wy *STHA* RG19 ....24 C3
Inkpen Rd *HUNG* RG17 ....16 D5
  HUNG RG17 ....18 A3
Irish Hill Rd *HUNG* RG17 ....18 B3

J

Jedburgh Cl *STHA* RG19 ....25 F2
Jesmond Dene *NWBY* RG14 ....2 A2
John Hunt Cl *STHA* RG19..........25 E3
Jonathan Hi *KSCL* RG20...........28 D5
Jubilee Rd *NWBY* RG14 ....2 E6
Junction Ter *NWBY* RG14..........3 G5
Justice Cl *STHA* RG19 ....25 F3

K

Keeps Md *KSCL* RG20 ....43 E3
Keighley Cl *STHA* RG19 ....24 C3
Kelvin Rd *NWBY* RG14 ....2 E2
Kempton Cl *NWBY* RG14 ....23 E4
Kendal Cl *NTHA* RG18.............24 C1
Kendrick Rd *NWBY* RG14 ....27 H3
Kennedy Cl *NWBY* RG14 ....27 H2
Kennet Cl *STHA* RG19 ....25 E2
Kennet Rd *NWBY* RG14 ....2 C1
Kennet Side *NWBY* RG14 ....3 G4
Kennett Pl *NWBY* RG14 ....2 C1
Kennet Wy *HUNG* RG17............16 C1
Kersey Crs *NWBY* RG14 ....12 A5
Kestrel Cl *STHA* RG19 ....24 B2
Kevin Cl *KSCL* RG20 ....43 H4
Kiln Dr *NTHA* RG18 ....7 G2
Kiln Rd *NWBY* RG14 ....13 E5
Kiln Ter *NWBY* * RG14 ....7 G2
Kimbers Cl *NWBY* * RG14 ....2 B4
Kimbers Dr *NWBY* RG14 ....11 G5
Kingfisher Ct *NWBY* RG14 ....3 J4
King John Rd *KSCL* RG20..........43 F4
Kingsbridge Rd *NWBY* RG14 ......22 A4
Kingsland Gra *NWBY* RG14 ....22 A5
Kingsley Cl *NWBY* RG14...........12 D5
Kings Rd *NWBY* RG14 ....2 D5
Kings Rd West *NWBY* RG14 ....2 D5
Kintbury Sq *HUNG* RG17 ....18 A3
Kipling Cl *NTHA* RG18............14 C5
Knightsbridge Dr *STHA* RG19......30 B5
Knights La *KSCL* RG20 ....26 A5
Knowle Crs *KSCL* RG20 ....43 F4

L

Laburnum Gv *NWBY* RG14 ....2 C1
Ladwell Cl *NWBY* RG14 ....27 H3
Lamb Cl *NTHA* RG18 ....14 C5
Lambourn Rd *KSCL* RG20 ....11 G4
Lambourn Valley Wy
  KSCL RG20 ....11 F2
Lamp Acres *NWBY* RG14 ....12 D5
Lancaster Cl *HUNG* RG17..........16 B4
  NTHA RG18.............24 C1
Lancaster Sq *HUNG* RG17 ....16 C4
Larch Cl *NWBY* RG14 ....11 H5
Larch Dr *KSCL* RG20 ....43 F4
Larkspur Gdns *NTHA* RG18 ....25 F1
Laud Cl *NWBY* RG14 ....13 F5
The Laurels *NTHA* * RG18 ....14 C5
Lawrence Md *HUNG* RG17 ....18 A3
Lawrences La *NTHA* RG18..........14 D4

Layland's Gn *HUNG* RG17 ....
Layleys Gn *NTHA* RG18 ....
Leonardslee Crs *NWBY* RG14 .....
Leslie Southern Ct *NWBY* RG14 ...
Lewendon Rd *NWBY* RG14 ....
Leys Gdns *NWBY* RG14 ....
Lime Cl *NWBY* RG14 ....
Limes Av *KSCL* RG20.............
Limetree Av *KSCL* RG20..........
Lincoln Ct *NWBY* RG14 ....
Linden Cl *NWBY* RG14 ....
Lindenmuth Wy *STHA* RG19 ....
The Lines *KSCL* RG20 ....
Lingfield Rd *NWBY* RG14.........
Link Rd *KSCL* RG20 ....
  NWBY RG14 ....
Link Vw *NWBY* * RG14 ....
Link Wy *NTHA* RG18 ....
Lipscomb Cl *NWBY* RG14 ....
Lipscombe Cl *NWBY* RG14 ....
Lisle Cl *NWBY* RG14 ....
The Litter *KSCL* RG20 ....
Little Knowle Hi *KSCL* RG20.....
Livingstone Rd *NWBY* RG14 ......
London Rd *NTHA* RG18 ....
  NWBY RG14 ....
  STHA RG19 ....
Longacre *NWBY* RG14 ....
Long Cl *HUNG* RG17 ....
Longcroft Rd *KSCL* RG20.........
  STHA RG19 ....
Long Gv *THLE* RG7 ....
Long La *NTHA* RG18 ....
  NWBY RG14 ....
Longmead *KSCL* RG20 ....
Loundyes Cl *NTHA* RG18 ....
Love La *KSCL* RG20..............
  STHA RG19 ....
Lower Farm Ct *STHA* RG19 ....
Lower Wy *STHA* RG19 ....
Ludlow Cl *NWBY* RG14............
Lyon Cl *STHA* RG19 ....

M

Macklin Cl *HUNG* RG17 ....
Madeira Pl *NWBY* RG14...........
Magpie Cl *STHA* RG19 ....
Main St *STHA* RG19..............
Majendie Cl *NWBY* RG14 ....
Malham Rd *STHA* RG19 ....
Mallard Ct *NWBY* RG14 ....
The Maltings *NWBY* RG14 ....
Malvern Ct *NWBY* RG14...........
Mandarin Cl *NWBY* * RG14 ....
Manor La *NTHA* RG18.............
Manor Pl *NWBY* RG14 ....
Mansell Dr *NWBY* RG14 ....
Maple Crs *NWBY* RG14............
Marchant Cl *STHA* RG19 ....
Marconi Rd *NWBY* RG14 ....
Market St *NWBY* RG14 ....
The Marlowes *NWBY* RG14.........
Marlston Rd *NTHA* RG18 ....
Marshalls Ct *NWBY* RG14 ....
Marsh La *HUNG* RG17 ....
  NTHA RG18.............
  NWBY RG14 ....
Marsh Rd *NTHA* RG18 ....
Marston Dr *NWBY* RG14 ....
The Martins *STHA* RG19..........
Masefield Rd *NTHA* RG18 ....
Matchlock Ms *NWBY* * RG14 ......
Matthews Cl *STHA* RG19 ....
Mayfair Dr *NWBY* RG14 ....
Maynard Cl *NTHA* RG18 ....
Mayors La *NWBY* RG14 ....
Mayow Cl *STHA* RG19 ....
Meadow Cl *STHA* RG19 ....
Meadow Rd *NWBY* RG14...........
Meadowsweet Cl *NTHA* RG18 ......
Medway Cl *NTHA* RG18............
Meldrum Cl *NWBY* RG14 ....
Mersey Wy *NTHA* RG18 ....
Meyrick Dr *NWBY* RG14 ....
Middle Cl *NWBY* RG14 ....
Middleton Ct *NWBY* RG14 ....
Middletons Cl *HUNG* RG17........
Milkhouse Rd *KSCL* RG20.........
Mill Bank *HUNG* RG17............
Millgreen La *STHA* RG19 ....
Mill La *KSCL* RG20 ....
  NWBY RG14 ....
Mill Reef Cl *STHA* RG19 ....
Ministry Rd *STHA* RG19..........
Monks La *NWBY* RG14.............

swood Cl *NWBY* RG14 ....27 H1
acute Dr *STHA* RG19............25 F3
ague Ter *NWBY* RG14............22 C4
gomery Rd *NWBY* RG14 ......22 A2
ment Cl *NWBY* RG14............27 H1
e's Pl *HUNG* RG17............16 B3
La *NWBY* RG14............22 A2
oors *STHA* RG19............24 D3
y Pl *HUNG* RG17............16 C3
ount *NWBY* RG14............22 C5
batten Cl *NWBY* RG14............13 E5
t Cl *KSCL* RG20............32 D5
BY RG14............22 C4
t Rd *KSCL* RG20............32 D4
............24 D1
e Marsh *STHA* RG19............25 G2

N

y Ri *NWBY* RG14 ....13 F5
e Dr *STHA* RG19............25 E2
old Rd *NWBY* RG14............11 H5
olt Cl *NTHA* RG18............14 C5
ury Rd *KSCL* RG20............42 D3
RG18............8 A1
ury St *HUNG* RG17............18 B3
ort Cl *NWBY* RG14............3 F2
ort Rd *NWBY* RG14............3 F2
d *NWBY* RG14............2 E7
............29 F1
own Rd *NWBY* RG14............22 C4
gan Cl *STHA* RG19............24 D2
ghtingales *NWBY* RG14............22 D5
ds *NTHA* RG18............14 C5
a Ri *NWBY* RG14............27 C3
rook St *NWBY* RG14............2 C5
croft La *NWBY* RG14............2 A3
croft Ter *NWBY* RG14............2 B4
ern Av *NWBY* RG14............12 C4
field Rd *NTHA* RG18............24 B1
St *KSCL* RG20............43 F4
view *HUNG* RG17............16 C5
way *NTHA* RG18............14 C5
BY RG14............2 E6
wood Dr *NWBY* RG14............3 G1
Cl *NWBY* RG14............27 G2

O

KSCL RG20............43 G4
NWBY RG14............2 A6
Gv *NWBY* RG14............21 H5
Cl *HUNG* RG17............16 C3
lds Cl *KSCL* RG20............41 H2
nds *NTHA* RG18............7 E4
y Rd *NWBY* RG14............3 J1
dge Cl *NWBY* RG14............22 A5
 re Rd *STHA* RG19............25 E3
llows Rd *NWBY* RG14............2 B5
th Rd *NWBY* RG14............2 B2
RG20............19 E4
wtown Rd *NWBY* RG14............2 B7
chard *STHA* RG19............23 H2
dene *NWBY* RG14............3 F2
rd Park Cl *HUNG* RG17............16 C4
ecks *NWBY* RG14............3 J2
ridge Sq *NWBY* RG14............23 G2
Rd *NWBY* RG14............12 D4
s Gv *NWBY* RG14............3 J2
d Rd *NWBY* RG14............2 B1
St *HUNG* RG17............16 D1
RG14............2 B2

P

ddock *KSCL* RG20............43 E4
RG14............3 H5
ck Rd *NWBY* RG14............22 B4
gs La *KSCL* RG20............32 D5
NTHA RG18............24 D1
nd *NWBY* RG14............2 D2
KSCL RG20............19 H4
RG18............14 D5
le Rd *NTHA* RG18............14 C1
HUNG RG17............16 D3
Y RG14............2 C2
r *NWBY* RG14............2 C2
y *HUNG* RG17............16 C4
age La *HUNG* RG17............16 B2
Cl *NWBY* RG14............22 A3

Pavy Cl *STHA* RG19............25 F3
Paynes Cl *STHA* RG19............37 E3
Paynesdown Rd *STHA* RG19............24 B2
Peachey Dr *STHA* RG19............25 F3
Pearces Pl *KSCL* * RG20............43 F4
Pear Tree La *NWBY* RG14............13 C5
Peckmoor Dr *STHA* RG19............29 E5
Peel Gdns *KSCL* RG20............43 E3
Pegasus Cl *STHA* RG19............24 A1
Pelican La *NWBY* RG14............2 C2
Pembroke Rd *NWBY* RG14............2 D2
Penn Rd *NWBY* RG14............11 H5
Penny's Hatch *KSCL* RG20............43 G4
Penrose Cl *NWBY* RG14............12 D5
The Pentlands *HUNG* RG17............18 C3
Penwood Hts *KSCL* RG20............33 E3
Penwood Rd *KSCL* RG20............27 G5
Phoenix Ct *KSCL* RG20............43 F4
Pigeons Farm Rd *STHA* RG19............29 F1
Pike St *NWBY* RG14............3 F1
Pimpernel Pl *NTHA* RG18............25 F1
Pinchington La *NWBY* RG14............28 D1
Pindar Pl *NWBY* RG14............13 G5
Pine Rdg *NWBY* RG14............13 E5
Pinewood Dr *NWBY* RG14............34 C1
Pipers Ct *STHA* * RG19............25 C3
Pipers La *STHA* RG19............25 F4
Pipers Wy *STHA* RG19............25 C5
Pipit Cl *STHA* RG19............24 B2
Plantation Cl *NTHA* RG18............7 H2
Plumpton Rd *NWBY* RG14............23 E4
Poffley Pl *STHA* RG19............25 G2
Pond Cl *NWBY* RG14............27 H1
Popes Hl *KSCL* RG20............43 E4
Poplar Pl *NWBY* RG14............12 C5
Poppy Dr *NTHA* RG18............25 F1
Porchester Rd *NWBY* RG14............22 C4
Porlock Cl *STHA* * RG19............24 D3
Porter End *NWBY* RG14............22 D5
Posting House Ms
    NWBY RG14............22 A1
Pound La *KSCL* RG20............34 A5
    NWBY RG14............21 H1
    STHA RG19............24 A2
Pound St *NWBY* RG14............2 B6
Poveys Md *KSCL* RG20............43 G4
Prancing Horse Cl *STHA* RG19............25 E2
Preston Pl *NWBY* RG14............13 F5
Prince Hold Rd *STHA* RG19............24 A2
Priors Cl *KSCL* RG20............43 F4
Priors Court Rd *NTHA* RG18............8 A1
Priory Av *HUNG* RG17............16 C4
Priory Cl *HUNG* RG17............16 C4
Priory Pl *HUNG* RG17............16 C4
    NWBY RG14............28 D2
Priory Rd *HUNG* RG17............16 C4
    NWBY RG14............22 C4
Pritchard Cl *STHA* RG19............29 F1
Prospect Pl *NWBY* RG14............2 C7
Prospect Rd *HUNG* RG17............16 C3
Puffers Wy *NWBY* RG14............22 A3
Pyle Hl *NWBY* RG14............22 D4

Q

The Quantocks *STHA* RG19............24 D3
Quarrington Cl *STHA* RG19............25 E3
Queens Cl *KSCL* RG20............43 G4
    NWBY RG14............2 E6
Queens Wy *HUNG* RG17............18 B3

R

Railway Rd *NWBY* RG14............2 E5
Ramsbury Dr *HUNG* RG17............16 D3
Ramsbury Ter *HUNG* RG17............16 D3
Rectory Cl *NWBY* RG14............2 A7
Redfield Ct *NWBY* RG14............3 K2
Red Shute Hl *NTHA* RG18............8 A3
Reed Wk *NWBY* RG14............3 G1
Regent Cl *HUNG* RG17............16 C1
Regents Ct *NWBY* RG14............2 C2
Regnum Dr *NWBY* RG14............12 D5
Remembrance Rd *NWBY* RG14............22 A3
Richmond Av *STHA* RG19............24 A2
The Ridge *NTHA* RG18............14 C1
The Rise *NTHA* RG18............14 C2
River Pk *NWBY* RG14............3 F3
River Wk *NWBY* RG14............2 C2
Robertsfield *STHA* RG19............23 H2
Robertson Cl *NWBY* RG14............22 D5
Robins Cl *NWBY* RG14............28 B1
Rockingham Rd *NWBY* RG14............2 A5

Roebuts Cl *NWBY* RG14............22 B5
Rokeby Cl *NWBY* RG14............28 C1
Roman Wy *NTHA* RG18............24 A1
Rooksfield *KSCL* RG20............36 A1
Rookswood *KSCL* RG20............10 D4
Rope Wk *STHA* RG19............24 C3
Rosedale Gdns *STHA* RG19............24 C3
Rosier Cl *STHA* RG19............25 F3
Round End *NWBY* RG14............27 H3
Roundfield *THLE* RG7............15 H4
Rowan Dr *NWBY* RG14............12 D5
Roy Cl *NTHA* RG18............7 H1
Rudland Cl *STHA* RG19............24 D3
Rupert Rd *NWBY* RG14............22 B5
Russell Rd *NWBY* RG14............22 A3
Rydal Dr *STHA* RG19............24 A1

S

Saffron Cl *NWBY* RG14............2 B3
Sagecroft Rd *NTHA* RG18............14 C5
St David's Rd *NWBY* RG14............2 B5
St Donats Rd *STHA* RG19............24 D6
St George's Av *NWBY* RG14............2 A6
St John's Rd *NWBY* RG14............2 C7
    STHA RG19............24 C2
St Lawrence Sq *HUNG* RG17............16 C3
St Leger Cl *NWBY* * RG14............22 A1
St Marks Cl *STHA* RG19............24 C2
St Marys Paddock
    NTHA * RG18............14 C1
St Mary's Pl *NWBY* RG14............2 D2
St Mary's Rd *KSCL* RG20............43 F2
    NWBY RG14............2 D2
St Michael's Rd *NWBY* RG14............2 A6
St Nicholas' Rd *NWBY* RG14............2 B5
St Richards Rd *NWBY* RG14............12 D5
Salcombe Rd *NWBY* RG14............22 A4
Sanden Cl *HUNG* RG17............16 B3
Sandford Cl *NWBY* RG14............3 H4
Sandleford Pde *NWBY* * RG14............28 C1
Sandleford Ri *NWBY* RG14............28 C1
Sandown Wy *NWBY* RG14............23 E4
Sandpit Hl *KSCL* RG20............27 G5
Sandy Cl *NTHA* RG18............7 H3
Sandy La *NTHA* RG18............7 H3
Sargood Cl *STHA* RG19............25 E3
Sawmill Rd *NTHA* RG18............8 A3
Saxon Cl *STHA* RG19............24 A2
Sayers Cl *NWBY* RG14............22 D5
School La *KSCL* RG20............4 B3
Scrivens Md *STHA* RG19............25 F2
Second St *STHA* RG19............30 A4
Second St East *STHA* RG19............30 A3
Sedgefield Rd *NWBY* RG14............2 C5
Sedge Gv *NTHA* RG18............25 E1
Seventh St *STHA* RG19............29 H3
Severn Cl *NTHA* RG18............14 B5
Sewell Cl *NTHA* RG18............14 C1
Shakespeare Rd *NTHA* RG18............24 C1
Shalbourne Cl *HUNG* RG17............16 A3
Shaw Br *NWBY* * RG14............12 D5
Shaw Farm Rd *NWBY* RG14............12 D5
Shaw Hl *NWBY* RG14............12 D5
Shaw Rd *NWBY* RG14............2 E1
Sheepwash La *KSCL* RG20............34 C1
Shelley Rd *NTHA* RG18............24 C1
Sherrardmead *NWBY* RG14............12 D5
Shop La *NWBY* RG14............12 B4
Shrewsbury Ter *NWBY* * RG14............22 A4
Sidestrand Rd *STHA* RG19............21 H5
Simmons Fld *NTHA* RG18............25 F1
Sixth St *STHA* RG19............29 H3
Skilman Dr *STHA* RG19............25 F2
Skinner's Green La *KSCL* RG20............26 B2
    NWBY RG14............21 F5
Skippons Cl *NWBY* RG14............27 G2
Skylings *NWBY* RG14............3 G2
Slanting Hl *NTHA* RG18............8 A2
Smallridge *KSCL* RG20............27 G4
Smitham Bridge Rd
    HUNG RG17............16 B3
Snake La *KSCL* RG20............11 E4
Snowdon Cl *STHA* RG19............24 D3
Snowdrop Copse *NTHA* RG18............25 F1
Somerset Cl *HUNG* RG17............16 B3
Somerton Gv *STHA* RG19............24 C3
Sorrel Cl *STHA* RG19............13 F5
Southdown Rd *STHA* RG19............23 H2
Southend Rd *NTHA* RG18............14 C4
South Rd *KSCL* RG20............43 G4
South Vw *HUNG* RG17............16 C3
South View Gdns *NWBY* RG14............2 E2
Spackman Cl *STHA* RG19............24 D3
Spa Meadow Cl *STHA* RG19............29 E1
Speedwell Wy *NTHA* RG18............25 F1

Speen Hill Cl *NWBY* RG14............22 A1
Speen La *NWBY* RG14............22 A1
Speen Lodge Ct *NWBY* RG14............22 A1
Speen Pl *NWBY* RG14............22 A1
Spencer Rd *NWBY* RG14............27 H2
Spriggs Cl *STHA* RG19............24 D3
Springfield La *NWBY* RG14............22 C5
Springhurst *NWBY* * RG14............22 D5
Spring La *KSCL* RG20............34 B5
    NTHA RG18............14 C2
Spurcroft Rd *STHA* RG19............24 D3
The Square *STHA* RG19............30 A4
Stable Ct *NWBY* RG14............12 D5
Stanley Rd *NWBY* RG14............2 E6
Stapleton Cl *NWBY* RG14............27 G2
Star La *KSCL* RG20............32 D5
The Starting Ga *NWBY* RG14............3 G7
Station Ap *NWBY* RG14............2 C5
Station Rd *KSCL* RG20............32 D1
    NWBY RG14............2 C6
    NWBY RG14............11 H5
    STHA RG19............24 D2
Stephenson Cl *NTHA* RG18............24 D1
Stirling Wy *NTHA* RG18............24 C1
Stirrup Pightle *NWBY* RG14............28 D1
Stone Copse *NTHA* RG18............13 G3
Stoney La *NWBY* RG14............13 F4
    STHA RG19............25 E2
Strawberry Hl *NWBY* RG14............2 B2
Strokins Rd *KSCL* RG20............43 F3
Strongrove Hl *HUNG* * RG17............16 B2
Stroud Gn *NWBY* RG14............2 E7
Strouds Meadow *NTHA* RG18............14 C3
Stuart Rd *NWBY* RG14............27 G2
Sunderland Pl *NTHA* RG18............24 C1
Sunley Cl *NWBY* RG14............27 H2
Sunnyside *KSCL* * RG20............43 E5
Sutherlands *NWBY* RG14............28 A1
Sutton Rd *NWBY* RG14............11 H5
Swangate *HUNG* RG17............16 C1
Swan St *KSCL* RG20............43 E5
Sycamore Ri *NWBY* RG14............13 E4
The Sydings *NWBY* RG14............11 H5
Sydney Cl *STHA* * RG19............25 E2
Sylvester Cl *NWBY* RG14............12 A5

T

Tadham Pl *STHA* RG19............24 C3
Talbot Cl *NWBY* RG14............12 A5
Tamarisk Ct *NTHA* RG18............25 F1
Tarn Howes Cl *STHA* RG19............24 A2
Tarn La *NWBY* RG14............22 B5
Tarrant's Hl *HUNG* RG17............16 C1
Tealgate *HUNG* RG17............16 C1
Tennyson Rd *NTHA* RG18............24 C1
The Thakerays *STHA* RG19............24 D3
Thames Rd *NTHA* RG18............14 B5
Third St East *STHA* RG19............30 A3
Thirtover *NTHA* RG18............14 B1
Thompson Cl *NTHA* RG18............7 H1
Thompson Dr *STHA* RG19............25 E3
Thorneley Rd *KSCL* RG20............43 F4
Thornfield *STHA* RG19............30 D5
Thornford Rd *STHA* RG19............30 B4
Three Acre Rd *NWBY* RG14............22 B5
Titcombe Wy *HUNG* RG17............18 A3
Tomlin Cl *STHA* RG19............25 E3
Toomers Whf *NWBY* * RG14............2 C4
Town Mills *NWBY* * RG14............2 C4
Trade St *KSCL* RG20............32 B5
Trefoil Dro *NTHA* RG18............25 F1
Trent Crs *NTHA* RG18............14 B5
The Triangle *NWBY* RG14............28 D1
Trout Wk *NWBY* RG14............12 D5
Tubb's La *KSCL* RG20............32 D5
Tudor Rd *NWBY* RG14............2 D7
Tull Wy *NTHA* RG18............23 H1
Turners Dr *STHA* RG19............25 E2
The Turnery *STHA* RG19............24 D2
Turnfields *STHA* RG19............24 D2
Turnpike Rd *NTHA* RG18............23 G1
    NWBY RG14............3 K1
Two Rivers Wy *NWBY* RG14............3 K3
Tydehams *NWBY* RG14............28 A1
Tyler's La *THLE* RG7............9 H5
Tyne Wy *NTHA* RG18............14 B5

U

Ullswater Cl *STHA* RG19............24 A2
Union La *KSCL* RG20............43 F1
Uplands *HUNG* RG17............16 B3
Urquhart Rd *STHA* RG19............24 D4

V

Valley Rd *NWBY* RG14 ....**21** H5
Vanners La *KSCL* RG20 ....**26** B3
Vicarage La *NTHA* RG18 ....**14** C2
Victoria Gdns *NWBY* RG14 ....**2** D2
Victor Rd *STHA* RG19 ....**25** E2
Villiers Wy *NWBY* RG14 ....**27** G2
Vincent Rd *NTHA* RG18 ....**25** E1
Violet Gv *NTHA* RG18 ....**15** E5

W

Waldegrave Pl *NWBY* * RG14 ....**2** C4
Waller Dr *NTHA* RG18 ....**13** C5
Walters Cl *NTHA* RG18 ....**14** C2
Walton Wy *NWBY* RG14 ....**3** G2
Wansey Gdns *NWBY* RG14 ....**13** F5
Waram Cl *HUNG* RG17 ....**16** D1
Warehouse Rd *STHA* RG19 ....**29** H3
Warren Rd *NTHA* RG18 ....**27** H2
Warwick Dr *NWBY* RG14 ....**22** D4
Wash Water *KSCL* RG20 ....**27** E5
Water La *STHA* RG19 ....**23** E5

The Waverleys *NTHA* RG18 ....**24** D1
Weavers Wk *NWBY* * RG14 ....**2** C3
Webbs Acre *STHA* RG19 ....**25** F3
Wellhouse La *NTHA* RG18 ....**8** D1
Wellington Cl *NWBY* RG14 ....**13** E5
Wellmans Meadow *KSCL* RG20 .....**43** E3
Well Meadow *NWBY* RG14 ....**12** D5
Well St *KSCL* RG20 ....**34** C5
Wendan Rd *NWBY* RG14 ....**22** B4
Wenlock Wy *STHA* RG19 ....**24** D3
Wentworth Ct *NWBY* RG14 ....**2** E7
Wessex Cl *HUNG* RG17 ....**16** B3
Westbourne Ter *NWBY* RG14 ....**2** B1
Westbrook Cl *HUNG* RG17 ....**16** B3
Westerdale *STHA* RG19 ....**24** C2
Western Av *NWBY* RG14 ....**2** A1
Western End *NWBY* RG14 ....**22** A3
Westfield Crs *NTHA* RG18 ....**24** B1
Westfield Rd *NTHA* RG18 ....**14** A5
Westfield Wy *NWBY* RG14 ....**22** A5
Westgate Rd *NWBY* RG14 ....**22** A5
Westland *NTHA* RG18 ....**24** B1
Westlands Rd *NWBY* RG14 ....**22** C5
Westmead Dr *NWBY* RG14 ....**22** B5
West Mills *NWBY* RG14 ....**2** B4
West Mills Yd *NWBY* * RG14 ....**2** B4
Westridge *KSCL* RG20 ....**38** C2
West St *KSCL* RG20 ....**40** A2

NWBY RG14 ....**2** B3
Westwood Rd *NWBY* RG14 ....**23** E4
Wharf Rd *NWBY* RG14 ....**2** D4
Wharf St *NWBY* RG14 ....**2** C4
Wheatlands La *NWBY* RG14 ....**27** F2
Wheatsheaf La *NWBY* RG14 ....**3** F1
Wheelers Green Wy
  STHA RG19 ....**25** E3
Whitakers Cl *NTHA* RG18 ....**24** B1
White Cl *NTHA* RG18 ....**7** H1
White Hl *KSCL* RG20 ....**39** H4
  KSCL RG20 ....**41** H3
Whitelands Rd *NTHA* RG18 ....**24** C1
Wilfred Wy *STHA* RG19 ....**25** F2
William Cl *STHA* RG19 ....**24** D3
Williams Ct *HUNG* * RG17 ....**16** C2
Willis Cl *NTHA* RG18 ....**8** B4
Willow Cl *NWBY* RG14 ....**22** B4
Willowmead Cl *NWBY* RG14 ....**27** G3
Willow Rd *KSCL* RG20 ....**35** H1
Winchcombe Rd *NWBY* RG14 ....**2** D5
Windermere Wy *STHA* RG19 ....**24** A2
Windsor Ct *NWBY* RG14 ....**2** E4
Windsor Ri *NWBY* RG14 ....**23** E5
Winston Wy *STHA* RG19 ....**23** H1
Winterbourne Rd *KSCL* RG20 ....**4** C3
Winterton Dr *NWBY* RG14 ....**11** H5
Withybed Wy *NTHA* RG18 ....**15** E5

Wolsingham Wy *STHA* RG19 ....
Woodavon Gdns *NTHA* RG18 ....
Woodbine La *KSCL* RG20 ....
Woodlands *KSCL* RG20 ....
Woodlands Cl *NTHA* RG18 ....
Wood Rdg *NWBY* RG14 ....
Woodside *NTHA* RG18 ....
Woodside Dr *NTHA* RG18 ....
Woolton Lodge Gdns
  KSCL RG20 ....
Wordsworth Rd *NTHA* RG18 ....
Wormersley Rd *STHA* RG19 ....
Wurford Dr *STHA* RG19 ....
Wyndham Rd *NWBY* RG14 ....

Y

Yates Copse *NTHA* RG18 ....
Yeomans La *KSCL* RG20 ....
Yew Cl *KSCL* RG20 ....
Yew Ga *NWBY* RG14 ....
York Cl *NWBY* RG14 ....
York Rd *HUNG* RG17 ....
  NWBY RG14 ....
Young Crs *STHA* RG19 ....

Index - featured places

AFC Newbury
  NWBY RG14 .... 2 E3
Annie Lawson School
  NWBY RG14 .... 22 A4
Battlesite 1644
  NWBY RG14 .... 12 A5
Battlesite 1643
  NWBY RG14 .... 27 H1
Benham Park
  KSCL RG20 .... 21 E1
Berkshire Business Centre
  STHA RG19 .... 25 G3
Bone Lane Industrial Area
  NWBY RG14 .... 3 H3
Brockhurst
  Pre-Preparatory School
  NTHA RG18 .... 9 F3
Brockhurst School
  NTHA RG18 .... 9 G3
Brookway Industrial Estate
  NWBY RG14 .... 3 K5
Burghclere J & I School
  KSCL RG20 .... 34 C5
Castle Industrial Park
  NWBY RG14 .... 13 E5
The Castle Special School
  NWBY RG14 .... 12 B4
Cheam School
  STHA RG19 .... 36 D3
The Clere Secondary School
  KSCL RG20 .... 34 C4
Cold Ash St Marks CE
  Primary School
  NTHA RG18 .... 14 B1
Colthrop Business Park
  STHA RG19 .... 25 E2
Corn Exchange
  NWBY RG14 .... 2 C4
Croft Hall
  HUNG RG17 .... 16 C2
Curridge Primary School
  NTHA RG18 .... 7 F3
Denvale Trading Park
  NWBY RG14 .... 3 J5
Donnington Castle
  NWBY RG14 .... 12 A3
Donnington Valley
  Hotel & Golf Club
  NWBY RG14 .... 12 B2
Downe House School
  NTHA RG18 .... 8 A4
Dunston Park Infant School
  NTHA RG18 .... 24 D1
Enborne CE Primary School
  KSCL RG20 .... 26 C2
Falkland Memorial
  NWBY RG14 .... 27 H2
Falkland Primary School
  NWBY RG14 .... 27 H1
The Fieldgate Centre
  KSCL RG20 .... 43 E4

Fir Tree Primary School
  NTHA RG18 .... 23 G1
Francis Baily Primary School
  STHA RG19 .... 25 E2
Greenham Road Retail Park
  NWBY RG14 .... 2 D6
Grimsbury Castle
  NTHA RG18 .... 8 C2
Health Club & Swimming Pool
  STHA RG19 .... 3 K6
Highclere Castle & Gardens
  KSCL RG20 .... 39 F4
Horizon West Industrial Estate
  NWBY RG14 .... 3 K4
Horris Hill School
  KSCL RG20 .... 28 A5
Hungerford Community
  Health Clinic
  HUNG RG17 .... 16 B2
Hungerford Gallery
  HUNG RG17 .... 16 C3
Hungerford Leisure Centre
  HUNG RG17 .... 16 C5
Hungerford Primary School
  HUNG RG17 .... 16 C3
Hungerford Town FC
  HUNG RG17 .... 16 C4
Hungerford Trading Estate
  HUNG RG17 .... 16 A3
John O'Gaunt School
  HUNG RG17 .... 16 C5
John Rankin Infant School
  NWBY RG14 .... 21 H5
John Rankin Junior
  NWBY RG14 .... 21 H5
Kennet Leisure Centre
  STHA RG19 .... 25 E2
Kennet School
  STHA RG19 .... 25 E2
Kingfisher Court
  Industrial Estate
  NWBY RG14 .... 3 J4
Kingsclere CE
  Primary School
  KSCL RG20 .... 43 F4
Kingsclere Health Centre
  KSCL RG20 .... 43 F4
Kingsclere Park
  KSCL RG20 .... 43 E3
Kingsland Centre
  STHA RG19 .... 24 D2
Kintbury St Marys CE
  Primary School
  HUNG RG17 .... 18 B3
London Road Industrial Estate
  NWBY RG14 .... 2 E3
The Mary Hare Grammar
  School for the Deaf
  NWBY RG14 .... 6 B4
Meadowview Squash Club
  HUNG RG17 .... 16 D1

Mill Hall School
  STHA RG19 .... 23 G5
Newbury Business Park
  NWBY RG14 .... 3 G2
Newbury Bus Station
  NWBY RG14 .... 2 C5
Newbury College
  NWBY RG14 .... 28 C1
Newbury Cricket &
  Hockey Club
  NWBY RG14 .... 2 A3
Newbury & Crookham
  Golf Club
  STHA RG19 .... 29 C1
Newbury District Hospital
  NWBY RG14 .... 2 A7
Newbury Racecourse
  STHA RG19 .... 3 K7
Newbury Retail Park
  NWBY RG14 .... 28 D1
Newbury RFC
  NWBY RG14 .... 28 B2
New Greenham Park
  KSCL RG20 .... 30 A3
New Greenham Park
  Leisure Centre *KSCL* RG20 .... 30 A3
Norland College
  HUNG RG17 .... 17 H1
Northcroft Leisure Centre
  NWBY RG14 .... 22 A2
Oakley Farm Caravan &
  Camping Park
  KSCL RG20 .... 27 H5
Park House School
  NWBY RG14 .... 28 A2
Parsons Down Infant School
  STHA RG19 .... 24 A2
Parsons Down Junior School
  STHA RG19 .... 24 A2
Pipers Industrial Estate
  STHA RG19 .... 25 F4
Raceview Business Centre
  NWBY RG14 .... 3 F5
Red Shute Hill
  Industrial Estate
  NTHA RG18 .... 8 A2
Ridge House
  Pre-Preparatory School
  NTHA RG18 .... 14 D2
Rivermead Industrial Estate
  STHA RG19 .... 25 H4
Riverpark Industrial Estate
  NWBY RG14 .... 3 G3
Robert Sandilands
  Primary School
  NWBY RG14 .... 22 A1
St Bartholomews School
  NWBY RG14 .... 22 A4
St Finians RC Primary School
  NTHA RG18 .... 14 D2

St Gabriels School
  KSCL RG20 ....
St John the Evangelist
  Infant School
  NWBY RG14 ....
St Joseph RC Primary School
  NWBY RG14 ....
St Marys CE Junior School
  NTHA RG18 ....
St Michaels School
  KSCL RG20 ....
St Nicholas CE School
  NWBY RG14 ....
St Nicolas CE Junior School
  NWBY RG14 ....
St Thomas Infant School
  KSCL RG20 ....
Shaw Cum Donnington
  Primary School
  NWBY RG14 ....
Snelsmore Common
  Country Park
  NWBY RG14 ....
Speenhamland Primary School
  NWBY RG14 ....
Spurcroft Primary School
  STHA RG19 ....
Station Road Industrial Estate
  STHA RG19 ....
Station Yard Industrial Estate
  HUNG RG17 ....
Sterling Industrial Estate
  NWBY RG14 ....
Stockcross Primary School
  KSCL RG20 ....
Thatcham Bowling Club
  NTHA RG18 ....
Thatcham Business Village
  STHA RG19 ....
Thatcham Town FC
  STHA RG19 ....
Thornford Park Track
  STHA RG19 ....
Thorngrove School
  KSCL RG20 ....
Trinity School
  NWBY RG14 ....
Turnpike Industrial Estate
  KSCL RG20 ....
Watermill Theatre
  NWBY RG14 ....
West Berkshire Museum
  NWBY RG14 ....
Whitelands Park Primary School
  NTHA RG18 ....
Winchcombe J & I School
  NWBY RG14 ....
Woolton Hill Junior School
  KSCL RG20 ....

Notes

Notes

AA **Street by Street** QUESTIONNAIRE

Dear Atlas User
Your comments, opinions and recommendations are very important to us.
So please help us to improve our street atlases by taking a few minutes
to complete this simple questionnaire.

You do NOT need a stamp (unless posted outside the UK). If you do not want to remove this page from your street atlas, then photocopy it or write your answers on a plain sheet of paper.

Send to: The Editor, AA Street by Street, FREEPOST SCE 4598,
Basingstoke RG21 4GY

ABOUT THE ATLAS...

Which city/town/county did you buy?

Are there any features of the atlas or mapping that you find particularly useful?

Is there anything we could have done better?

Why did you choose an AA Street by Street atlas?

Did it meet your expectations?

Exceeded ☐   **Met all** ☐   **Met most** ☐   **Fell below** ☐

Please give your reasons

continued overleaf

Where did you buy it?

For what purpose? (please tick all applicable)

To use in your own local area ☐   To use on business or at work ☐

Visiting a strange place ☐   In the car ☐   On foot ☐

Other (please state)

LOCAL KNOWLEDGE...

Local knowledge is invaluable. Whilst every attempt has been made to make the information contained in this atlas as accurate as possible, should you notice any inaccuracies, please detail them below (if necessary, use a blank piece of paper) or e-mail us at *streetbystreet@theAA.com*

ABOUT YOU...

Name (Mr/Mrs/Ms)

Address

                                                    Postcode

Daytime tel no

E-mail address

Which age group are you in?

Under 25 ☐   25-34 ☐   35-44 ☐   45-54 ☐   55-64 ☐   65+ ☐

Are you an AA member?   YES ☐   NO ☐

Do you have Internet access?   YES ☐   NO ☐

Thank you for taking the time to complete this questionnaire. Please send it to us as soon as possible, and remember, you do not need a stamp (unless posted outside the UK).

ML